UNKNOWN
CAMBRIDGE

UNKNOWN CAMBRIDGE

Secret Stories from Cambridge, Town and Gown

MALCOLM HORTON

FIRST EDITION

ISBNs

978-1-80227-624-4 (eBook)
978-1-80227-625-1 (paperback)

ACKNOWLEDGEMENTS

I would like to thank the following for their help in discovering some of Cambridge's lesser known tales. The late Charles Larkham , Bursar of Sidney Sussex College, Dr Genny Silvanus, College Archivist, Christ's College. Jenny Ulp, College Archivist, Downing College. John Wagstaff, Librarian, Christ's College. Chris Skilton of Cambridge Tour Guides. Carol Lamb of the Fitzwilliam Museum. Staff of the Cambridge Folk Museum. The late Professor Shon Ffowks-Williams, Master of Emmanuel College (1996-2002). The late Dennis Flanders FBA, RWS, John Doyle MBE, PPRWS, Dennis Roxby Bott RWS. Catherine Twilley, Development Director, Christ's College. Simon Bradley, Editor of Pevsners Cambridgeshires. Charles Brooking, Architectural Historian.

CONTENTS

INTRODUCTION

The purpose of this book is to highlight aspects of Cambridge not usually mentioned in the conventional guide books. Featuring the eccentric, bizarre and outrageous people who have lived and passed through this beautiful and unique city.

But first, with the reader's indulgence, I would like to paint a conventional backcloth to the origins and history of Cambridge, both town and gown. In that way, the reader can be reminded that these strange tales are not set in some fictional fantasy world.

It is difficult to believe that the borough of Cambridge did not attain the full title and dignity of a city until March 1951, 400 years after Oxford. It received a Borough Charter from King John in 1201 and the university was established in 1209. However, because of its location away from the pathway of kings and armies on their way to London, Cambridge has always been essentially provincial. In the view of many, Cambridge is pre-eminent in Britain as a city of fine architecture and wonderful landscapes (the Backs).

The first settlements in Cambridge from the Iron Age were on the north side of the river and it is where the Romans settled. As you climb the first part of Castle Hill from Magdalene Bridge to Mount Pleasant, a distance of just over 300 yards, you have traversed old Cambridge.

The main reason for choosing Castle Hill, as is explained in the first story, is the commanding view it affords of the surrounding countryside, making it more defensible against hostile predators. Also, the Romans in particular never built on flood plains. However, it was not until the arrival of the Normans in the 11th century that a castle was built on top of the mound.

CASTLE HILL CAMBRIDGES FIRST SETTLEMENT .NORTH OF CAM

It was with the arrival of, first, the Anglo-Saxons after the departure of the Romans in 410 AD, that the centre of Cambridge began to move to the other side of the river, a process accelerated by the invasion of the Vikings in 875

AD for who, being seafaring folk, building on flood plans was of no concern.

Old Cambridge fell into disrepair and the wonderful Roman buildings disappeared as the move to the south of the River Granta gained momentum. Today, there are few signs of old Cambridge, particularly as the university developed on the south side of the Granta, which, in turn, became the River Cam.

Cambridge's association with the early development of the United States of America is pivotal. Its early settlers included scholars like John Harvard, who founded a world-famous university, and the Washington family whose coat of arms is the basis of the American flag with its stars and stripes.

Perhaps the greatest invention of all time, electrical conduction, was the brainchild of Granville Wheler of Christ's College and Stephen Gray. The Chinese poet Xu Zhimo whilst at King's wrote what many think is the finest Cambridge poem, "Saying Goodbye to Cambridge Again".

Cambridge is the birthplace of Association Football (soccer) where, in 1863, the first rules were devised. The father of the Jet Age, inventor Sir Frank Whittle, created the jet engine whilst a student at Peterhouse. The legendary rock group Pink Floyd and their eccentric founder Syd Barrett were Cambridge-based in their early years. Morse creator, Colin Dexter, was a Cambridge man, Christ's College, who created the legendary Oxford detective. The Fitzwilliam is home to the paintings of the British artist who may have been Jack the Ripper.

The list is endless and reveals many tales unearthed for the first time.

OLD CAMBRIDGE – THE ROMAN CONNECTION (70 AD)

The departure point for most travellers by road from both Oxford and Cambridge is Magdalen Bridge (the Cambridge version has an e on the end).

However, in the case of Cambridge, it is the exit point from new Cambridge and the entry point to old Cambridge, the Roman Duroliponte.

As you climb the first part of Castle Hill from the end of Magdalene Street to Mount Pleasant, a distance of just over 300 yards, you have traversed old Cambridge. There are no boundary markers or signs because Duroliponte has been consigned to the mists of time, and yet at the time of the Roman occupation, this had been the very centre of Cambridge and had been since the Iron Age.

The reason for choosing Castle Hill, or more particularly the mound which sits on top of the hill, is the commanding view it afforded of the surrounding countryside, thus making it more defensible against hostile predators. Also, the Romans always built their forts above flood plains. It was not a major fort for the Romans, otherwise it would have had "chester" added to its name, like Great Chesterford and Godmanchester, which were nearby.

Old Cambridge covered an area of less than twenty-five acres but was close to an important crossing point over the River Granta (later to be renamed the Cam).

After the Romans left in 410 AD, the fine buildings they had erected in Duroliponte gradually fell into decay. The incoming Viking tribes, in any case, were settling on the other side of the river because, being seafaring folk, flood plains were not a concern.

When the Normans came, they consolidated the defensive qualities of old Cambridge by building a castle on top of the mound; a wooden structure initially, and then stone a few years later. It stood the test of time still being in use at the time of the English Civil War (1642–1648). All this time, Cambridge's centre of gravity was moving in a southerly direction back across the newly named River Cam, and old Cambridge virtually disappeared from the face of the map.

So, what remains of old Cambridge? Precious little, unless you are particularly eagle-eyed.

What remains from the Roman period is to be found in the mediaeval church of St Peter built in the 12th century, a short way up Castle Hill. In its structure are long, flat, reddish Roman roof tiles, or *tegulae*, and on the south side Roman bricks, both used along with flint and clunch (chalk) found locally.

The Romans were not hampered by the lack of good quality building stone in the Cambridge area. They used manufactured bricks, kiln-fired bricks and tiles from local clay, a craft which departed from British shores along with the Romans in 410 AD. So, when new buildings were required, the Roman buildings were pulled down and their materials used to build the newer but inferior structures. It was to be a thousand years before the art of brick and tile making was to be reintroduced to Cambridge by Flemish and Dutch craftsmen, as witnessed by Queens' College (1448), Christ's College (1505) and St John's College (1511), which are all largely of brick construction.

Another more tangible structure from the Norman period is Merton Manor, built in the 12th century for a Norman nobleman and which was bought by Merton College, Oxford, along with the adjoining School of Pythagoras, not long after their construction. Situated at the bottom of Castle Hill, they were purchased from Merton by St John's College in 1959, and are Cambridge's oldest continuously occupied dwellings.

One of the oldest hostelries in Cambridge was the 16th century White Horse Inn at the foot of Castle Hill. It closed in 1934 and reopened as the acclaimed Folk Museum in 1936, a permanent reminder of old Cambridge or Duroliponte.

MERTON HALL AND THE SCHOOL OF PYTHAGORAS CAMBRIDGES OLDEST DOMESTIC
BUILDINGS BELONGED TO MERTON COLLEGE OXFORD FROM 1200 INTIL 1959
WHEN IT WAS ACQUIRED BY ST JOHNS COLLEGE CAMBRIDGE

FOLK LORE MUSEUM

THE GLOMERALS SEED OF CAMBRIDGE UNIVERSITY (CIRCA 1200)

Asking a Cambridge student or a college fellow where you might find the Master of Glomery, or indeed the Glomerals, would cause much head scratching and cynicism. You would probably be recommended to consult the Harry Potter works of fiction, or indeed Barbara Euphan Todd's Worzel Gummidge books.

The rather dissonant sounding noun "glomeral" is, in fact, a corruption of the word "grammar", i.e. Latin, and a much lower class of student who came to Cambridge before there was a university, solely to pick up a smattering of Latin in order that he might pursue the profession of schoolmaster.

They were akin to the boys attending monastic and cathedral schools specifically to learn Latin to carry out their duties as choristers, and Cambridge possessed many monastic schools, long before the foundation of the university.

The Glomerals were answerable to the Master of Glomery who, in turn, was appointed by the Archdeacon of Ely Cathedral, even after the establishment of the University of Cambridge in 1209. Their school, Glomery Hall, was situated in Glomery Lane (now St Mary's Lane) on land now occupied by the eastern end of King's College Chapel.

They were admitted to the lesser degree of Master of Glomery. They lived a hard, hand to mouth existence and had no permanent abode and were often forced to beg.

Even after the establishment of Cambridge University, its chancellor had no jurisdiction over them, which remained the prerogative of the Master of Glomery and his boss, the Archdeacon of Ely and, ultimately, the Bishop of Ely.

With the establishment of the university and its scholars, the Glomerals were greatly disesteemed, and considered a blot on the academic landscape.

So, in 1430, the celebrated "Processus Barnwellensis", confirmed by a papal bull by Pope Eugenius IV, transferred the power of the Bishop of Ely and his officials over the School of Glomery, and as a result the post of Master of Glomery, to the chancellor of the university, and by 1442, the Glomerals seemed to have disappeared into the mist of time, as though they had never existed.

CAMBRIDGE'S DEBT TO WOMEN FOUNDERS (1336)

The first sixteen Cambridge colleges were founded between 1284 and 1596. Six of them were founded by six wealthy women, and one of these had three joint women founders: Queens', between 1448 and 1484.

The second Cambridge foundation was Clare College in 1336, which was also the first to be founded by a woman, Elizabeth Countess of Clare, a granddaughter of Edward I. She had been widowed three times before she was thirty and was an extremely wealthy woman, and so could afford to generously endow her new college.

The third Cambridge college founded was Pembroke in 1347 by a friend of the Countess of Clare, the widowed Countess of Pembroke, Marie de Valence. She was only seventeen when she married the fifty-year-old Earl of Pembroke, who died of apoplexy three years later.

The third female foundation was Queens', initially founded by Queen Margaret of Anjou in 1448. Her husband, Henry VI, founded King's in 1441. However, the Wars of the Roses and the defeat of the weak

Lancastrian Henry VI threatened the future not only of his own King's College, but also his wife's foundation, Queen's. Fortunately, the new Yorkist King Edward IV had a wife, Elizabeth Woodville, who was keen to support the continuation of Queen's College and not only supported it financially but obtained its first statutes. The involvement of a second queen was not officially recognised until 1831 when the apostrophe in Queen's was repositioned to after the s, to become Queens', in the plural. It is not generally realised that a third successive queen was involved, Queen Anne Neville, wife of the controversial Yorkist, King Richard III. She not only supported Queens' financially, she also arranged for the college to use Richard III's heraldic badge, the boar's head, as its second heraldic device.

The fourth female foundation was Christ's College, which was richly endowed by Lady Margaret Beaufort, mother of the first Tudor monarch, Henry VII, who famously defeated Richard III at the Battle of Bosworth. Lady Margaret was an extremely wealthy woman, having outlived four wealthy husbands, and as a result was Countess of Richmond and Countess of Derby. She also founded St John's College in 1511. She was an extremely devout and pious woman whose confessor, John Fisher, was a leading Cambridge theologian and largely instrumental in persuading Lady Margaret to found her two colleges. Recent historians have cast her in a somewhat controversial light, implying that her piety was, in effect, penitence for her part in putting her son on the English throne, including removing the Princes in the Tower, always attributed to Richard III. But that's another story.

The sixth female founder was Frances Sidney, Countess of Sussex, who in 1596 founded Sidney Sussex College on land leased from Trinity College. To achieve this security of tenure, she enlisted the help of her friend, Elizabeth I, who with a little arm-twisting persuaded the authorities of Trinity to grant the Countess of Sussex a lease in perpetuity at a rent of twenty marks annually. After all, the Queen's father founded Trinity. Incidentally, this rent of twenty marks (£13.33) is still paid to this day.

What is remarkable about women founding university colleges at this time was that women were not even allowed a university education at Oxbridge until the 19th century, and were not awarded degrees until 1920 at Oxford and 1948 at Cambridge.

MARGARET BEAUFORT SECOND FOUNDATION ST JOHNS COLLEGE. THE DINING HALL
WITH PORTRAIT OF LADY MARGARET ABOVE HIGH TABLE

THE EAGLE'S UNIQUE FASCINATION, DNA PIONEERS, WARTIME HEROES AND GHOSTS (1353)

The Eagle is undoubtedly Cambridge's oldest hostelry still extant. It dates from the 14th century and was known as The Eagle and Child for many centuries. Coincidentally, there is a hostelry in Oxford called The Eagle and Child.

Jonathan Weiner's *Long for This World* asserts that a tavern stood on The Eagle site in 1353, with beer at three gallons a penny.

Records indicate that Corpus Christi College owned the site in 1566 when it granted a lease for forty years at an annual rent of £3 6s 8d.

By the 18th century, it was a coaching inn with a service leaving from London, Charing Cross every night in the early evening at 5:30 p.m., and arriving at The Eagle at 3 a.m. Coaches, in turn, left for London every evening at 6 p.m. However, the arrival of the railway in Cambridge in 1845 quickly led to the demise of The Eagle's stagecoach service.

The Eagle is probably most famous for the proclamation to the whole world on 28th February 1953 that scientists from the nearby Cavendish Laboratory had discovered the "secret of life"; the discovery of DNA. The two scientists concerned, Francis Crick and James Watson, no doubt became suitably inebriated.

Apart from the announcement of DNA, The Eagle is probably most famous for its RAF bar, whose ceiling is covered in graffiti of British and American World War Two pilots who burnt their names and squadron numbers with lighters, candles and cigarettes. They can still be seen plainly to this day, thanks to painstaking restoration carried out by former RAF technician James Chainey. There were no less than twenty-six British and American airfields around Cambridge.

No pub story would be complete without its resident ghost tale and The Eagle is no exception.

In the mid 17th century, a mother sleeping in one of the rooms set light to her bedclothes by accidentally knocking over a candle in her sleep. Her three children were unable to escape because the door was locked and the window would not open, and so they perished. The fate of the mother is not recorded. However, ever since the unfortunate incident, that particular window is always left open, summer and winter, day and night. On the rare occasion it has been shut, the ghosts of the children have not been able to escape and the whole pub is imbued with a suffocating sensation like smoke from a fire. Therefore, the window, which is above the garden courtyard, is always kept open so the ghosts of the children can escape.

So seriously does the landlord take this phenomenon, that a clause is included in the lease requiring said window to always be kept open.

One fascinating story was related to me by Chris Skilton of Green Badge Tour Guides, who related how quite recently one of his most venerable guides was telling the ghost story to a group, with the window behind her. She noticed they were looking puzzled. When Janet turned round, she saw the window was shut. She immediately went inside and informed the staff, who were horrified as they have strict instructions to keep the window open. A few days later, they had an electrical fire and only just caught it in time. So, the window is now nailed open. Be sure to check when you next visit The Eagle!

TOP LEFT WINDOW LEFT PERMANENTLY OPEN TO ALLOW CHILDRENS GHOSTS TO ESCAPE.

CEILING OF BAR OF EAGLE ADORNED BY GRAFFITI FROM SECOND WORLD WAR AIRMEN.

FOUR HUNDRED YEARS OF ELITISM (1441)

The first half of the 14th century saw a tremendous expansion of new college foundations in Cambridge: seven in all, culminating with Pembroke College in 1347. In the next ninety years, only two new colleges were founded.

This sudden slowdown in college foundation was due to two factors: the Black Death, which reduced the population in England by 40% (one and a half million), and the ruinously expensive Hundred Years' War with France.

Then, in 1441, that hapless and mentally handicapped monarch Henry VI founded King's College, a twin foundation with Eton which he had founded a year earlier in 1440. The idea being that students of his school at Eton in Berkshire would progress on to King's to complete their education. He had intended to found King's at Oxford, which after all is much nearer, but the spiritual climate prevailing at Oxford was, at that time, uncongenial due to the polemical writings of John Wycliffe and others, translators of the Bible into English and precursor to the Protestant Reformation. Henry VI was a very devout Catholic, so he chose to set up his university college at Cambridge.

He called his new college King's and it was to be the grandest of all the colleges in Oxford and Cambridge, which, of course, it is with the unequalled grandeur of King's College Chapel.

However, the university authorities were not happy with the discriminatory nature of Henry's new foundation, open only to scholars from Eton College. This elitism was to last for 400 years and it was not until 1873 that non-Etonians were admitted. Further disquiet was caused when King's students were granted special privileges. They were awarded degrees without sitting university examinations, and were not subject to the discipline of the university authorities.

Henry VI, a Lancastrian, was defeated in the Wars of the Roses in 1471 when he was killed. He was succeeded by the Yorkist Edward IV.

He was a weak monarch who achieved very little, losing both the Wars of the Roses and England's last territories in France (with the exception of Calais), but he will be remembered for founding two of England's most famous seats of learning.

HENRY VIII'S GRANDMOTHER –
CAMBRIDGE'S GREATEST BENEFACTOR (1509)

The late 15th century saw many of the early educational institutions in Cambridge falling into decay, particularly Michaelhouse (later absorbed into Trinity) and God's House. The cause was the double whammy of the Black Death (1347–1353), which wiped out 40% of the English population, and the ruinously expensive Hundred Years' War with France (1337–1453).

John Fisher, Bishop of Rochester, had been a student at God's House and enlisted the help of Lady Margaret Beaufort to resurrect it as Christ's College. Lady Margaret was the controversial mother of Henry VII, the first Tudor monarch, who defeated Richard III at the Battle of Bosworth in 1485, effectively bringing to an end the Wars of the Roses in favour of the House of Lancaster.

Lady Margaret was one of the wealthiest women in late mediaeval England, having outlived four wealthy husbands, and was as a result Countess of Richmond and Derby. She had only one child, Henry, who spent his formative years exiled in France before returning to become king.

She was, in later life, a devout and pious woman who, in 1497 at the age of fifty-four, chose as her confessor John Fisher, and together this formidable pair founded Christ's College in 1505, and St John's College in 1511 (completed posthumously two years after Lady Margaret's death in 1509). She was not only wealthy, she was very thrifty, and lived a life of abrogation, wearing a hair shirt next to her skin in place of all the regal fineries of her rank. She established at both Oxford and Cambridge the first endowed professorships in divinity, which are named after her. John Fisher was the first holder of the position in Cambridge in 1497 followed by the Dutch theologian Erasmus in 1511.

Despite her enormous contribution to the advancement of learning, her greatest legacy was her single-minded determination to put her Welsh son Henry on the throne of England by fair means or foul. Henry was the product of her second marriage to Owen Tudor, so he was a direct descendant from John of Gaunt, Duke of Lancaster, both on his mother and father's side by virtue of John of Gaunt's two marriages, and thus a Lancastrian. But enough! That's another story.

CAMBRIDGES GREATEST BENEFACTOR LADY MARGARET BEAUFORT . A RARE
EXAMPLE OF HER SIGNATURE (TOP LEFT)FROM A CHRIST'S COLLEGE FOUNDATION
DOCUMENT ,WITH HER SEAL ATTACHED ,FROM 1506.SHE WAS HENRY V11S MOTHER.

MALTON 21 Hen.VII

Letter of Attorney from the Lady
Margaret to receive Manor from Henry
Hornby et al. This document has a
particularly fine seal and is one of
the few documents with the Foundress's
signature.   E.A.C.

ENDOWMENT DOCUMENT

THE TREASONABLE BUCKINGHAMS AND MAGDALENE COLLEGE (1521)

Magdalene College Cambridge has not always been so-named. It started life in 1428 as Monk's Hostel, a Benedictine foundation to cater for the educational needs of the abbeys of Ely, Ramsey, Walden and Crowland, all local to the area.

The lead was taken by Abbot Lytlington of Crowland, who obtained letters patent from King Henry VI to acquire a six-acre site on the western side of the River Cam adjacent to Cambridge's first bridge, over what was then known as the River Granta.

It was Cambridge's first college to be founded on the western side of the Cam, ostensibly to avoid the temptations of town life.

Monk's Hostel was not well-endowed and utilised existing buildings on the site. In short, it was badly in need of a benefactor, and one appeared in the shape of Henry Stafford, second Duke of Buckingham, in 1470.

Abbot Crowland and Buckingham together planned First Court and began building a much-needed chapel, and each of the abbeys represented at Monk's Hostel built their own accommodation blocks.

In recognition of Henry Stafford's financial support, the college was named Buckingham College. But in 1483, Buckingham was executed for treason for leading the Buckingham Rebellion against Richard III.

An explanation is needed here to explain the relationship of the Stafford family (first Duke of Buckingham) to the participants in the Wars of the Roses, the Houses of Lancaster (red rose) and York (white rose).

Buckingham was a descendant of Edward III (1322–1377), fifth son of Thomas of Woodstock, whose brothers included John of Gaunt, Duke of Lancaster, and Richard, Duke of York, whose sons were the main protagonists in the Wars of the Roses (1455–1485).

In "The Cousins' War", the Staffords were key supporters of the Lancastrian cause and Henry Stafford lost first his father and then grandfather in 1455 and 1460, in the Battle of St Albans and Battle of Northampton, respectively. The latter was won by Edward, Duke of York who, as a result, succeeded to the English crown as Edward IV.

The young Henry Stafford, aged only eight, was made ward to the new king and overnight became a Yorkist, and aged eleven was married off to the king's sister-in-law Catherine Woodville.

He was an extremely wealthy young man, as well as being a cousin of the king. When Edward IV died unexpectedly, he became an enthusiastic supporter of the king's brother, the future Richard III, the controversial suspect in the death and disappearance of the Princes in the Tower. The basis of Richard's claim to the throne was the assertion that his elder brother was illegitimate and had no right to the crown in the first place.

Such a well-supported claim would have encouraged the Duke of Buckingham to stake his own claim to the throne and hence "The Buckingham Rebellion" of 1483, which failed. This resulted in Buckingham's conviction and execution for treason, and the confiscation of his title and lands. Naturally, work at Buckingham College ceased.

However, the Buckingham family's titles and lands were restored two years later when his Tudor cousin Henry Tudor usurped Richard III in the Battle of Bosworth, becoming Henry VII.

However, it was not until 1519 when Edward, the third Duke of Buckingham, took up his father's patronage of the eponymous Buckingham College and it was he who built the college's hall.

His patronage, however, was short-lived because he too was executed for treason under somewhat dubious circumstances in 1521. The reason seems to have been his aristocratic disdain for the lowly born Cardinal Wolsey, Henry VIII's chancellor. Henry did not impede Wolsey's revenge because it conveniently removed a potential threat: the Staffords were of Plantagenet lineage, dating back to Henry II.

Work once again stopped at Buckingham College.

It would be a further twenty years before another potential patron arrived and the college changed its name to Magdalene.

But that's another story.

THE ENGLISH CRADLE OF PROTESTANTISM (1525)

The church of St Edward King and Martyr is located somewhat obscurely on Peas Hill in central Cambridge, just behind the market.

It is one of only five churches in England dedicated to the Anglo-Saxon king, Edward (959 AD–978 AD), who ruled for only three years before he was murdered by his stepmother, Queen Aelfthryth, on the steps of Corfe Castle. She stabbed him while he was leaning from his horse, partaking of a cup of wine. The purpose of removing her stepson was to secure the throne for her natural son by her second marriage, the five-year-old Ethelred.

The present church dates from the 13th century but is on the site of a much older Anglo-Saxon church, but 400 years later, the church gained more notoriety as the cradle of the Protestant religion in England. It was where, on Christmas Eve 1525, Cambridge graduate Robert Barnes preached his first openly evangelical sermon accusing the Catholic church of heresy.

In 1511, the arrival of the Dutch philosopher Erasmus in Cambridge was the catalyst for greater interest in the Protestant writings of the German philosopher Martin Luther. Amongst Erasmus' pupils during his two-year stay at Cambridge's Queens' College were Hugh Latimer, Nicholas Ridley and Thomas Cranmer, all to be early adherents to the Protestant faith.

Robert Barnes' Cambridge sermons soon attracted the attention of Cardinal Wolsey who was busy burning Martin Luther's books and other writings. Barnes was summoned to London to answer charges of heresy, but escaped to Antwerp in 1528 when he was warned the authorities were planning his execution. He reached Wittenburg in 1530 where he studied under Martin Luther.

Barnes returned to England when Thomas Cromwell, a fierce Protestant, became the new Chancellor of England in succession to the disgraced Thomas Wolsey. Henry VIII had now turned to the Protestants to help him by sanctioning his divorce from Catherine of Aragon, but Martin Luther (whose opinion was sought) could not approve. So, Henry ceased to favour their cause.

When Thomas Cromwell later fell from grace over Henry's disastrous marriage to Anne of Cleves, Barnes lost his protector and he was burnt for heresy in 1540.

However, Robert Barnes will always be remembered for his key role in establishing the Protestant faith in

England and his keynote sermon at the church of St Edward King and Martyr on 24th December 1525.

CAMBRIDGE'S GOLDEN AGE OF POLITICAL INFLUENCE (1533–1660)

Henry VIII was determined to divorce his wife of twenty-four years, Catherine of Aragon. The Roman Catholic church and even the Protestant reformer, Martin Luther, opposed such a plan; even his Chancellor, Thomas Wolsey, was averse to such a suggestion. So, the latter was removed to be replaced by the ardent Protestant Thomas Cromwell. At the same time, 1533, Thomas Cranmer, another committed Protestant, was appointed Archbishop of Canterbury.

Cranmer was a graduate of Jesus College Cambridge and whilst an undergraduate, he became a disciple of the Dutch Protestant philosopher Erasmus, who was the Lady Margaret Professor of Divinity residing at Queens' College from 1510–1515.

It was Thomas Cranmer, in a moment of divine afflatus, who suggested to Henry VIII a way out of his little local difficulty with Rome: why not consult your learned men at your great universities, without waiting for the inevitable delays and anticipated rejection of the Papal Court?

Oxford University would not give Henry the answer he wanted, so it was to the wise men of Cambridge that he turned. After much jiggery-pokery, they gave him the answer he desired.

As a result, there arose in Cambridge the grandest of foundations, Trinity College, Henry VIII's gift to Cambridge for its cooperation.

For the next 100 years, Cambridge was to outrank its great rival, Oxford, in the hold over the nation's affairs, with the likes of Burghley, Walsingham, Cranmer, Parker, Whitgift and Oliver Cromwell holding sway.

THE FOUR HUNDRED AND SEVENTY YEARS OF FIEFDOM OF MAGDALENE COLLEGE (1542)

Magdalene College Cambridge was originally founded in 1428, as Monk's Hostel, by Abbot Lytlington of Crowland Abbey, for student monks of the Benedictine order from the nearby abbeys of Crowland, Ely, Walden and Ramsey. By 1483, it had become known as Buckingham College, in recognition of the financial support provided by the second and then the third Dukes of Buckingham.

After the execution of these two dukes, in 1483 and 1521 respectively for treason, it would be another twenty years before, in 1541, another benefactor arrived on the scene, courtesy of the process known as the "Dissolution of the Monasteries", part of Henry VIII's Reformation.

The so-called benefactor was Thomas Audley, Baron Audley, Henry VIII's chancellor, and Buckingham College was his reward for presiding over the trial and execution of Anne Boleyn. He also disposed of Sir Thomas Moore, John Fisher (Bishop of Rochester) and finally Thomas Cromwell, bringing him even greater rewards.

In the two years prior to his death in 1544, he changed the name of the college to St Mary Magdalene and gave it fresh statutes which prescribed that he and his descendants should in perpetuity be the college's Visitor, who would have sole power to appoint the college's Master.

Baron Audley's only contribution to the well-being of his college was to settle in the college's favour a seven-acre piece of land in Aldgate, London which produced a rental income of £9 a year.

Even this apparent act of generosity was made with the expectation that when the universities and colleges went the same way as the monasteries as part of the Reformation, Audley would soon recoup his gift of Aldgate's seven acres.

His expectations were posthumously about to come to fruition, when in 1567 an Act of Parliament was passed requiring the universities and schools, like the monasteries earlier, to be dissolved and asset-stripped.

Henry VIII was on his deathbed, but his queen, Catherine Parr, persuaded him to change his mind and preserve England's great seats of learning. After all, he himself had founded one of the grandest colleges of all, Trinity Cambridge in 1546, just three years earlier.

But the rich and powerful magnates surrounding

Henry had persuaded a king weakened by illness to satisfy their hunger for more dissolution spoils. Fortunately, Catherine Parr proved a wiser counsel.

Audley's tenure lasted only two years before he too "popped his clogs". He had no children so the ownership of the college passed to a cousin, the Duke of Norfolk, who, in 1568, became the third benefactor to be executed for treason in less than 100 years.

Whilst all this was going on, an unscrupulous London banker, Benedict Spinola, in 1574 succeeded in seducing the master and fellows into permanently alienating the Aldgate land to the Crown in return for an increased rent from £9 to £15 a year. In 1580, Spinola sold the land to the Duke of Oxford for £2,500!

The original transaction with Magdalene College was thought by many to be illegal and was contested on more than one occasion.

The first lawsuit, pursued by Barnabas Goche (master 1604–1626), landed him and the senior fellow in prison for two years. When Goche was offered £10,000 to compromise, he refused. However, more than 400 years later in 1989, Magdalene erected a gargoyle representing Spinola designed by Peter Fluck and Roger Law, the creators of *Spitting Image*. Posterity will exact its own revenge: the gargoyle is for all to see on the quayside across the Cam from the main part of Magdalene College.

Finally, in 2012, Baron Audley's descendant, Lord Baybrooke, gave up his family's fiefdom of Magdalene College. The fellows now democratically elect the master, although the Audley descendants are still the college's Visitor. But this post is largely ceremonial containing no actual powers.

QUEEN CATHERINE PARR – THE TRUE FOUNDER OF HENRY VIII'S TRINITY COLLEGE (1546)

In Trinity Hall at Trinity College hangs a portrait of Catherine Parr, the sixth and surviving wife of Henry VIII. Their marriage was short-lived, 1543 until 1547 when Henry died.

However, her influence over the ageing king was profound because he greatly respected her wise and intelligent counselling; she was a master of rhetoric but one who also had a practical streak.

She was, in reality, the real founder of Trinity College in 1546, when she persuaded Henry to found a college in his name which would be the grandest of all the colleges in Oxford and Cambridge.

She became involved after an Act was passed in 1545 to dissolve the colleges of Oxford and Cambridge, in the same manner as that of the monasteries. The courtiers who had been fleshed by the spoils of the monasteries, like "wolves agape" as Archbishop Parker wrote, were baying for the possessions of the scholars.

The scholars petitioned Queen Catherine Parr to intervene, on their behalf, with King Henry. She persuaded him not only to spare these great seats of learning, but to use the spoils from the dissolved monasteries to found a royal college of unprecedented size and magnificence which would immortalise his name forever, and like King Alfred before him, show him as a great patron of learning.

Who could refuse such an invocation? Certainly not Henry VIII with his great ego, and in fairness, he was a man of great learning.

So, Henry combined two existing colleges, King's Hall and Michaelhouse, and seven hostels to form the grandest college ever and to this day it is by far the richest of all the Oxford and Cambridge colleges.

Up until that time, five of Cambridge's sixteen mediaeval colleges had been founded by women. In truth, she was effectively the sixth and that is why her portrait hangs in Trinity Hall just to the side of the High Table.

PARKER'S PIECE - SPORTING CONNECTIONS (1561)

Parker's Piece is a twenty-five-acre public park in the centre of Cambridge close to Downing College. It has three claims to national and international sporting fame.

The first, which has been dealt with in story number thirty-three in this volume, is the place where in 1863 men from Trinity College drew up the rules governing Association Football (soccer). These were known as the Cambridge Rules and codified the various types of football and separated it from rugby. And thus was born "the beautiful game". In the same year, the Football Association was inaugurated, which largely adopted the Cambridge Rules. As the Cambridge University Football Club claims to be the oldest football club in the world, it would seem wholly appropriate that soccer should have its parturition in Cambridge; the second claim to fame.

The third claim to fame is that Parker's Piece was the place where England's greatest cricketer, Jack Hobbs (1882–1963), learnt to play cricket. He was a local lad;

his father was groundsman and umpire at Jesus College. One of twelve children, he lived in great poverty, but took great delight as a child watching cricket at Jesus College. He practised day and night at Parker's Piece and played both cricket and football there for a local boys' team.

He played for Cambridgeshire a few times where he was spotted by the Surrey cricket legend Tom Hayward who, in 1901, took a Surrey cricket team to play at Parker's Piece against a Cambridgeshire team which included the young Jack Hobbs.

Hayward was so impressed that he persuaded Jack to move to Surrey, so he could qualify to play for the county team, which he did for thirty years. Known as the Master, Jack Hobbs is one of the greatest batsmen in the history of cricket. He is the leading run scorer and century maker in first class cricket; from 1905 to 1934, he scored 61,237 runs and 197 centuries. He represented England in Test matches on sixty-one occasions, scoring 15 centuries and averaging 56.94.

Jack Hobbs was knighted in 1953 and died in 1963.

Parker's Piece was originally owned by Trinity College until 1561, when it was swapped by Trinity for a piece of land owned by Cambridge Town Council, on which Trinity subsequently built the Wren Library. It is named after Edward Parker, a farmer who leased his eponymous twenty-five acres prior to the change of ownership. He was also a Trinity College cook.

It has hosted numerous great public events, including a dinner for 15,000 guests to celebrate Queen Victoria's coronation in 1838 and a rather smaller one to mark that of Edward VII.

In 1848, the university team moved to a new and more secure home, Fenners.

Today, Parker's Piece is a gigantic picnic area where people play informal games of cricket and football. To complete the amenity area, a big wheel has been installed, so there's a definite fairground feel to Parker's Piece especially with a number of pubs and restaurants running along the side.

PARKERS PIECE WHERE JACK HOBBS LEARNT TO PLAY CRICKET

THE BIRTH OF THE SECRET SERVICE (1570)

Mention the "Cambridge Spies" and thoughts immediately turn to Burgess, Philby and Maclean, the Soviet spies radicalised at Cambridge in the 1950s. These were traitors and enemies of the state.

However, it is not generally realised that in the reign of Elizabeth I (1558–1603), four Cambridge graduates played a crucial part in the setting up of the very first counter-intelligence spy network in the world. It was the forerunner of MI5 and MI6. They were the good guys, defending Elizabeth I and the realm against the very real threats of harm to the queen's person and possible invasion, particularly from Spain.

The four Cantabrigians were William Cecil (St John's), Francis Walsingham (King's), Thomas Phelippes (Trinity) and, to a lesser extent, the playwright Christopher Marlowe (Corpus Christi).

But first, it will be necessary to explain the unprecedented circumstances that gave rise to these desperate measures.

The years from 1545 to 1603, spanning the reigns of Henry VIII's children, were deplorable times for a nation divided between Protestantism and Catholicism. The boy king, Edward VI, who succeeded his father (Henry VIII) was a fanatical Protestant. He attempted to remove every vestige of Catholicism from the realm in the wake of his father's break with Rome and the creation of the Protestant Church of England. Edward's tutor had been the great Cambridge theologian and Greek scholar John Cheke, who was an ardent supporter of the Protestant teachings of Martin Luther in Europe. He also tutored Edward's sister, the future Queen Elizabeth.

If Edward's was a reign of terror for the Catholic population, what followed after his death in 1553 was even worse because his sister Mary, a staunch Catholic, succeeded him to the throne and immediately began terrorising the Protestant population with the same ritual executions and ceremonial burnings at the stake, to say nothing of the routine torture. She earnt the soubriquet "Bloody Mary".

Leading Protestants went into voluntary exile and their number included John Cheke and his pupil Francis Walsingham.

When Mary died in 1558, with the accession to the throne of her Protestant sister Elizabeth, the pendulum swung back again and the Catholics were, once again, persecuted.

Although his children had become polarised religiously, Henry VIII was not. He had set up the Protestant Church of England, not for religious reasons, but as a means of breaking with Rome in order to secure his divorce from the Catholic Catherine of Aragon, and his principal interest in closing Catholic monasteries was not religious but of a more pecuniary nature pelf. Their riches were diverted to the royal purse. The fact is that Henry VIII to his dying day was a Catholic.

However, he had sown the seeds of mistrust, hatred and fear. So, it was necessary to remove all potential threats to the incumbent monarch, both at home and overseas.

For Elizabeth I, there was the added problem of the Catholic Mary Queen of Scots who was rejected by the Scots and sought exile in England as a "guest" of her cousin Elizabeth. She was, literally, a cuckoo in the nest and the focal point of Catholics, not only in England but, more importantly, in Spain. The Spanish had other reasons to depose the English monarch, because of her encouragement of English buccaneers who were plundering their ships. So, plots to remove Elizabeth and replace her with Mary Queen of Scots were rife.

It was against this background that the queen's principal advisor, William Cecil, started the process of recruiting spies to keep the English monarch apprised of possible plots against her. It was not long before

Cecil delegated these extra duties to his friend, Francis Walsingham who was, in effect, Foreign Secretary and was without doubt a fanatical Protestant. He quickly recruited an army of spies both in England and Europe. He was ruthless and started recruiting double agents, mostly from the ranks of foreign spies who were facing death sentences and in return for being spared, "turned".

Not only spies were used, but codebreakers and forgers were utilised to great effect, particularly Thomas Phelippes, a brilliant codebreaker. There was also an operator, Arthur Gregory, who could open letters and reseal them without detection.

A young student at Corpus Christi, Christopher Marlowe, was forced to frequently visit Europe to spy in return for not being prosecuted for sedition in relation to his play *Tamburlaine*. It was such spies overseas who alerted Walsingham and Cecil about the imminent Spanish Armada invasion of Britain.

But the pinnacle of their success was the so-called Babbington Plot, when Walsingham's agents decrypted letters to and from Mary Queen of Scots conspiring against Elizabeth. As a result, Mary was tried and executed in 1587.

A year later, the Spanish Armada of 130 ships foundered in the English Channel, and thanks to Walsingham's effective spy network, England was prepared. It was due to his counter-intelligence apparatus that England was never again threatened with invasion, and went on to amass a global empire the likes of which had never before been witnessed.

Walsingham had done his job, and died two years later in 1590.

FRANCIS WALSINGHAM SPYMASTER

THE BACKS, WHERE COWS MAY SAFELY GRAZE (1574)

The area of land behind the college buildings which span the River Cam to the east of Queen's Road is known as the Backs. The colleges in question, St John's, Trinity, Trinity Hall, Clare, King's and Queens', are Cambridge's most prestigious, covering a distance of about one kilometre along the River Cam.

In this area, six college bridges span the Cam plus one public bridge, Garret Hostel Bridge. The Backs are, in effect, the gardens and meadows belonging to the six colleges spanning the Backs.

The Backs were, in 1995, listed by English Heritage as a Grade I Historic Park, and a former National Trust chairman, Simon Jenkins, has rated the view of the Backs towards King's College as one of the top ten in England. They are the reason why on comparing Cambridge with Oxford the former is referred to as being essentially pastoral while the latter is urban. The Backs cover an area of approximately fifty acres (twenty hectares).

As if to emphasise the soubriquet pastoral, every

spring local Red Pole cows appear on the western bank of the Backs area belonging to King's, where they have safely grazed for hundreds of years.

THE BACKS WHERE COWS MAY SAFELY GRAZE

The Backs were, until the 18th century, used largely by the colleges as a most convenient way of having goods delivered, especially heavy building materials and coal via the navigable River Cam.

Gradually, the amenity value of the Backs was realised with colleges laying out bowling greens and orchards.

But it was the employment by St John's in 1772 of landscape architect Capability Brown that really opened up the full potential of the Backs as gardens and pleasure areas, which proved most popular with the colleges' fellows, and other colleges soon followed suit.

One slightly alarming development over the years has been building development on the western side of the Backs due to improved drainage methods. Two colleges, St John's and Queens', have built quite substantial developments. One, St John's New Court, the "Wedding Cake", is truly beautiful, described by Nicholas Pevsner the architectural historian as the "fairy skyline". It was completed in 1831 and is certainly one of Cambridge's visual delights, whereas Queens' constructed more prosaic buildings in the 20th century, the Fisher building and the Lyons and Cripps Court.

However, these later developments have prompted tougher planning regulations and there is now a Tree Advisory Committee which meets regularly to discuss matters of common policy amongst the colleges along the Backs.

Hopefully, the above measures will ensure that this uniquely beautiful area will retain its green belt status as one of Cambridge's defining characteristics.

MARY, COUNTESS OF SHREWSBURY, CONTROVERSIAL BENEFACTOR OF ST JOHN'S (1592)

Between 1284 and 1594, the first sixteen Cambridge colleges were established and seven were founded by noblewomen. This despite the fact women were not admitted to Cambridge to study until the late 19th century.

However, an eighth woman, Mary Cavendish the Countess of Shrewsbury, was, by her enormous contribution to St John's College, effectively its joint founder along with Lady Margaret Beaufort, the mother of Henry VII. It's the Countess of Shrewsbury's statue which looks down from the eponymous Shrewsbury Tower at the far end of the Second Court, which she largely financed at the end of the 16th century. When work began, Mary had agreed to finance the total cost of the Second Court: £3,600 (equivalent to £62 million in today's money), but a series of self-inflicted vicissitudes circumscribed her contribution to £2,700.

Mary Cavendish was, at one time, an extremely wealthy and wilful woman blessed with good looks and used to getting her own way. But to fully appreciate both her circumstances and character, we must look to her mother, the illustrious Bess of Hardwick, her daughter's predecessor as Countess of Shrewsbury.

Bess of Hardwick, starting at the age of fifteen, was married no less than three times to extremely wealthy aristocrats, and by the time she was thirty-seven, had become one of the richest women in England, and such wealth allied to undoubted beauty made her one of the most desirable marriage prospects in the kingdom, after her third husband had died. So that when the sixth Earl of Shrewsbury came plighting his troth, she made part of the marriage bargain a condition that her youngest daughter from her first marriage, the twelve-year-old Mary Cavendish, should marry the earl's son, the prospective seventh Earl of Shrewsbury. Both marriages took place on the same day. By her series of marriages, Bess of Hardwick had moved up the aristocratic chain so as to end up being related to Henry VII and his mother, Lady Margaret Beaufort, the founder of St John's College.

Bess of Hardwick's aristocratic credentials were secured by her building Hardwick Hall and Chatsworth in Derbyshire, the latter being the seat of the Dukes of Devonshire who are descendants from her second marriage to Sir William Cavendish. Mary Queen of Scots was held under house arrest at Chatsworth by Bess' fourth husband the Earl of Shrewsbury, and she formed a firm friendship with her "house guest".

However, Bess' fourth husband died in 1592 and her daughter became Countess of Shrewsbury. Mary started emulating her royal relations and her mother by financing a prestigious building project, the Second Court at St John's. She then let her newly inherited status as wife of the seventh Earl of Shrewsbury go to her head and she gravely overstepped the mark by, first of all, converting to Roman Catholicism, which was bound to upset the Protestant King James I, and then in 1610, assisting her royal cousin Arabella Stuart in her elopement with William Seymour who was also Mary's cousin.

The problem with this intervention was that Arabella had been strictly forbidden to marry by King James because of the threat she posed, being fourth in line to the throne, and compounding the situation by converting to Roman Catholicism. Not only was that bad enough but her husband was sixth in line to the throne. It was clear that Mary knew exactly what the implications of her actions in assisting her cousin Arabella were and really did think she could get away with it, so to speak. But King James had no alternative but to consign her to the Tower of London from where, after five years, she was released in 1615 on compassionate grounds when both her husband and Arabella died in quick succession. Mary soon, however, found herself in hot water again when she refused to testify in an inquiry into the rumour that Arabella had produced a child from her union with William Seymour, pleading she had been sworn to secrecy. So, in 1623, she found herself back in the Tower of London where she remained until released in 1628.

On the occasion of each imprisonment in the Tower of London, she had been heavily fined and it was not surprising she was not able to find the balance of monies due on the building of St John's Second Court. However, she had covered 75% of the cost and that is why her statue was erected in 1672. She died in 1632 and was undoubtedly the most controversial of Cambridge's female benefactors.

COUNTESS OF SHREWSBURY ST JOHNS CONTROVERSIAL BENEFACTOR AND TOWER IN 2ND COURT WHICH BEARS HER NAME

A COLLEGE FOUNDED WITH A FIXED RENT FOR OVER 400 YEARS (1596)

Frances Sidney Countess of Sussex (1531–1589) was certainly well connected. Her father, Sir William Sidney, was Lord Chamberlain to Henry VIII's young son Edward VI, whilst her husband, Thomas Radcliffe third Earl of Sussex, occupied the same royal household job under Elizabeth I from 1572 until his death in 1583.

It was no surprise therefore that Frances Sidney was Lady of the Bedchamber to the young queen, advising on matters literary and musical.

Frances and Thomas Sussex had no children so in her will made after the death of her husband, Frances left £5000 (about £1 million in today's money) to found a new college at Cambridge to be called the Lady Frances Sidney Sussex College. It was to be a Protestant foundation on much the same lines as Emmanuel College Cambridge, founded by her neighbour and friend Walter Mildmay from Boreham in Essex. Again an acquaintance of great influence in the court of Elizabeth I, Chancellor of the Exchequer no less.

All of these connections were to prove extremely useful to Frances Sidney in her upcoming battle with Trinity College to secure land on which to build her new college.

St John's and Trinity had secured all the land in central Cambridge, particularly Henry VIII's Trinity College, which was the most prestigious ever founded, outranking Cardinal Wolsey's Christ Church College in Oxford and Henry VI's King's College in Cambridge.

Henry VIII acquired the resources and endowments of the numerous Catholic institutions he closed down in the Reformation, including many in Cambridge. He didn't actually need them all, but the powers that be at Trinity were reluctant to give up any of their spoils.

However, the executors of Frances Sidney's will, aided by her confessor William Whitgift, Archbishop of Canterbury, petitioned Queen Elizabeth, who after a little arm-twisting persuaded the Trinity men to hand over six acres of land previously occupied by the Greyfriars, suppressed by Henry VIII in 1546.

It was more or less derelict. Most of its buildings had been dismantled and the materials used in the building of Trinity.

A compromise was reached. Trinity would retain the freehold of the site and charge Frances Sidney's new college a rent of twenty marks (£13.33) a year in perpetuity.

The payment of this exact sum continues to this day.

An intriguing footnote concerning Frances Sidney's motives for founding a college in the first place remains.

A clue is perhaps given in her family motto, adopted by the college: "Dieu me garde de calomnie" meaning "God preserve me from calumny" i.e. false slander.

There was indeed a slander committed against her by a notorious Member of Parliament, Arthur Hall, who had laid his cap before the widowed lady only to have it rejected.

In one of his many spells detained in Fleet Prison for regular indiscretions, he wrote to Lord Burghley (Queen Elizabeth's chancellor) and Hall's stepfather, commenting that Lord Hunsden, who had succeeded to Frances Sidney's late husband's post as Lord Chamberlain, "had been Master of Games to Lady Sussex and hath lightened some of my lady's bags".

The mind boggles at the exact implications of these outrageous statements. Were they references to romantic attachments or financial assistance? Whatever, they were enough to have Frances Sidney excluded from the court of Queen Elizabeth.

Hence the good lady's attempt to restore her reputation and thus her legacy by founding a seat of learning. In addition, her will provided that on her death, a magnificent memorial be erected in St Paul's Cathedral. But her college, Sidney Sussex, continues to thrive and counts Oliver Cromwell as its most distinguished alumnus.

As for the scandal, nobody can quite recall what that was all about.

THE UNITED STATES OF AMERICA –
THE CAMBRIDGE CONNECTION (1630)

Henry VIII's Reformation, arising from his split with Rome and the foundation of the Church of England, led to the creation of Puritanism and the subsequent creation of the United States of America.

Puritanism was a religious movement whose initial aim was to remove all vestiges of Catholicism within the Church of England, and introduce a stricter moral code. Puritanism meant simpler church services, removing all the rituals and ceremonies not found in the Bible.

As a result, Puritans were much persecuted and even exiled to places like Holland, where their religious views were already "de rigueur".

One of the strongest strongholds of Puritanism was Suffolk and eastern England in general, and Cambridge University in particular. After all, Oliver Cromwell attended Sidney Sussex College.

The Puritans decided to set up a New England in

the New World of America, where they could create a sort of utopia and practise their religion and way of life unmolested.

The first settlement in America was Captain John Smith's Jamestown, Virginia in 1607, but this was in essence a totally commercial venture.

The second settlement was by the Puritan Pilgrim Fathers, who sailed from Plymouth, England in 1620 on the Mayflower to New England, to the north of Virginia. Amongst the 100 passengers was William Brewster, the only university-educated man in the party. He was a graduate from Peterhouse, Cambridge and became their religious leader until the arrival of another Cambridge man, the pastor Ralph Smith, who graduated from Christ's College.

The Pilgrim Fathers settled in what became Plymouth, Massachusetts. However, only half their number, fifty, survived the first harsh winter.

In 1630, the second wave of New England settlers established the Massachusetts Bay Colony in what is now Boston. The leader of this group of Puritan settlers was John Winthrop, yet another Cambridge graduate, from Trinity College. He laid out a network of highly organised towns, all named after English towns: Ipswich, Dedham, Salem, Chelmsford and New Town. Winthrop was the first governor of the colony and served for twelve years.

During the period of 1620 to 1640, 20,000 people migrated from England to New England.

New Town was to become even more famous when John Harvard, a graduate from Emmanuel College, Cambridge, died in Charlestown, Boston in 1638 and by his will left half of his estate, £800, and his valuable library to set up a university which was named after him, the eponymous Harvard University. His statue is a prominent feature in Harvard Yard.

New Town was renamed Cambridge in honour of yet another Cambridge graduate, the preacher Thomas Shepherd, but no doubt the authorities had in mind the enormous contribution Cambridge University had on the founding and development of New England.

New England and its four colonies: New Hampshire, Massachusetts, Rhode Island and Connecticut, were four of the thirteen colonies who signed the Declaration of Independence in 1776, which created the United States of America.

GEORGE DOWNING – HARVARD'S GIFT TO CAMBRIDGE (1642)

The First Court of Downing College, adjacent to the Porters' Lodge entrance, was completed in 2016 as part of a comprehensive development which includes the Heong Gallery and a refurbished building containing seventy-eight student rooms.

There is also, facing the student accommodation building, a memorial tablet which contains the following inscription:

> "Sir George
> DOWNING, *Bt*
> 1623–1684
> A. B. (Harv.) 1642
> Member of the
> First Graduating Class
> and Afterwards
> First Tutor of
> Harvard College

By dint of his personality,
diligence and industry
came the fortune of this
foundation"

One's first impression is that the memorial was in honour of the founder of Downing College, Sir George Downing, third baronet (1685–1749). However, when one examines the dates more closely one comes to the realisation that this was the founder's grandfather, another Sir George Downing.

The reason the grandfather is commemorated is that, as the memorial states, it was the residue of his fortune which was inherited by the founder and provided the wherewithal to start up the new Downing College in 1800. His fortune was amassed through lucrative appointments both governmental and diplomatic in the service of both Oliver Cromwell and Charles II. He was showered with material rewards for his many achievements, including a tract of land in Westminster on which he built the eponymous Downing Street, of which number 10 is the home to successive British prime ministers.

He is credited with instituting reforms to government finances which greatly increased the wealth of the Treasury, and carrying out reforms to Britain's maritime and military fleet which ensured its world supremacy for the next 200 years. He was a prominent spymaster whose smooth passage from the service of such disparate rulers,

Cromwell to Charles II, meant betraying former friends and colleagues of the discredited Cromwell regime. So, despite his great achievements, he remains a controversial figure.

However, Charles II rewarded him with not only material recognition but also created him a baronet. But although his grandson, the third baronet, officially founded Downing College, neither he nor his grandfather attended Cambridge University. However, the first baronet's father, Emanuel Downing (1585–1658) attended St John's College Cambridge and the second and fourth baronets attended Clare and Emmanuel Colleges, respectively.

What is most poignant is that Sir George Downing, first baronet, did attend a university in Cambridge, not in England but Massachusetts... the fledgling Harvard University, founded by John Harvard from Emmanuel College, Cambridge University, England. The young George Downing was one of the first batch of nine graduates from Harvard in 1642. He went on to become Harvard's first tutor.

George Downing's presence in Massachusetts was due to his father Emanuel being invited to the new colony by its first governor, John Winthrop, whose sister, Lucy, Emanuel had married. He took up a clerical and legal post in the new colony and remained there for nine years, before returning to Scotland with his family to take up a post as clerk to the council of Scotland. His son George pursued a career in government service, first as a soldier and then as a diplomat and Member of Parliament, as already explained. Another great achievement by George was to negotiate the transfer of New Amsterdam from the Dutch to England, which was then renamed New York. He also married into the powerful and aristocratic Howard family.

SIR GEORGE DOWNING 1ST BARONETS LEGACY

Not only was his alma mater, Harvard, named after John Harvard, a graduate of Emmanuel College Cambridge, England, but Cambridge, Massachusetts, where Harvard is situated, was named after Cambridge, England, after first being named New Town by the first English settlers in 1630.

Sir George Downing, the first baronet, is, in effect, Harvard University's gift to Cambridge University in gratitude for its foundation by John Harvard.

PAY SIXPENCE AND SEE CROMWELL'S HEAD (1660)

Oliver Cromwell's (1599–1658) association with Cambridge dates from 1616 when he was admitted to Sidney Sussex College. He left after one year to support his family, following his father's death. That association was renewed when he represented the town in Parliament from 1640–1649, having previously represented his hometown of Huntingdon from January 1628 to March 1629.

He was a Puritan who played a leading part in the English Civil War (1642–1651) on the side of the Parliamentarians against Charles I's Royalists, over the issue of who should govern Britain, the monarchy or Parliament.

Charles I (1600–1649) ascended to the United Kingdom throne in 1625 and, like his father James I, believed it was the divine right of kings to rule. This led him to frequently clash with Parliament, as he needed its approval to raise funds, particularly for his unsuccessful wars with France and Spain. "No taxation without representation" was Parliament's view.

So, in 1629, Charles I simply dissolved Parliament and ruled for eleven years without its interference, raising money through outdated taxes such as ship money. This approach greatly angered the population and nobles.

He eventually ran out of money and was forced to recall Parliament in 1640. Parliament immediately began introducing reforms, including the need for regular Parliaments and prohibiting the king from dissolving Parliament without its approval.

This led to the outbreak of the English Civil War in 1642. Though the Royalists, popularly known as the Cavaliers, won early victories, the Parliamentarians (known as the Roundheads on account of their puritanical short hair) eventually prevailed, with Oliver Cromwell playing a decisive part in the battles.

Charles I surrendered in 1648 and in January 1649, he was tried for high treason, found guilty and executed. Oliver Cromwell was one of the signatories on Charles I's death warrant.

The king's nineteen-year-old son Charles II escaped to Scotland where he raised an army that came south, and in 1651 fought Cromwell and his disciplined Model Army at Worcester, and was defeated. Charles II escaped and at one time evaded capture by famously hiding in an oak tree (The Royal Oak), but managed to reach France, where he remained in exile.

In 1653, in the absence of a monarchy, Oliver Cromwell was appointed Lord Protector and ruled in essence as a dictator, until his death from malaria in 1658. He was buried in Westminster Abbey alongside twelve English kings. Oliver Cromwell's son ruled briefly but lacked his father's leadership qualities and was removed from power by the army.

In 1660, Parliament, by popular consent, invited Charles II to return from exile in France to become monarch, but with Parliament ruling.

Almost his first act was to have Cromwell's body exhumed where it was then hanged and beheaded. His head was impaled on a pole in Westminster Hall where it remained for twenty years, until a great storm blew it down. His body was buried at Tyburn (roughly where Marble Arch is today) which was the principal place of execution for convicted traitors and religious martyrs.

Oliver Cromwell's head had a peripatetic career spending much of its time as a fairground attraction: "pay sixpence and see Oliver's head", and then became a collector's piece changing hands many times. Then in 1960, it was presented to his alma mater, Sidney Sussex College, by Dr H. N. S. Wilkinson whose family had owned it for over 100 years.

Its final resting place is somewhere in the antechapel of the chapel of Sidney Sussex. Its exact location is known only to those who witnessed its burial: the Master, three fellows and Dr Wilkinson. His death mask can be found in the Old Library, and there is, in the Senior Common Room, a pastel portrait by Samuel Cooper which, like Sir Peter Lely's famous portrait, shows Cromwell "warts and all". A very good oil painting of Oliver Cromwell from the late 17th century, by an artist unknown but after the style of Lely, hangs in the Hall. It is known to have belonged to Cromwell's son, Richard, and came into the possession of the college about seventy years ago as the gift of a master.

Incidentally, Oliver Cromwell was a descendant of Thomas Cromwell (1485–1540). He was Henry VIII's chief minister and was also parted from his head, by an ungrateful monarch, for arranging a disastrous marriage to Anne of Cleves.

However, Thomas Cromwell's descendant, Oliver Cromwell, changed forever the relationship between Parliament and the monarchy. Never again did the monarchy challenge Parliament's right to govern.

CHRISTOPHER WREN'S MASTERPIECE – ST PAUL'S CATHEDRAL AND THE CAMBRIDGE CONNECTION (1663)

The aftermath of the Great Fire of London in 1666 was Christopher Wren's rebuilding of St Paul's Cathedral. It elevated his status to that of a major architect to stand alongside his continental contemporaries. He was also commissioned to rebuild fifty-three city churches also destroyed by the Great Fire.

Wren had graduated in mathematics and physics in 1651 at Wadham College Oxford, before becoming a don at All Souls' College Oxford, and then being appointed Savilian Professor of Astronomy at Oxford in 1661.

Wren developed an interest in the new profession of architecture with its increasing emphasis on mathematics. Until this time, the design of buildings was carried out by the master stonemason or master carpenter. Buildings, however, were becoming more complex and classical due to the influences of the Italian Renaissance such as Baroque.

The building of the neoclassical chapel of Pembroke College in Cambridge was Wren's first major architectural design in 1662; a commission secured from his uncle, Matthew Wren, who was Master of Pembroke, whom we met in an earlier story.

Thus began Christopher Wren's illustrious career as an architect.

His second significant architectural project was the Sheldonian Theatre in Oxford with its striking cupola; a feature of the neoclassical buildings in Italy.

Its vast seventy-five feet by eighty feet ceiling required the application of detailed mathematical calculations, resulting in trusses hidden by the magnificent ceiling with thirty-two panels painted by Robert Streater. They help create Wren's concept of a Roman theatre, open to the sky.

The connection between London and Cambridge was William Sancroft, the Dean of St Paul's (1664–1668) and former President of Emmanuel College Cambridge (1662–1665). He became the seventy-nineth Archbishop of Canterbury in 1693.

Wren's early projects did not escape the notice of Sancroft who, in 1665, commissioned Wren to produce a programme of repairs and improvements to the old St Paul's Cathedral. His reluctance to leave Oxford had been overcome by Sancroft offering him the commission to rebuild Emmanuel College Chapel in the neoclassical style. This he commenced in 1667 and completed in 1673. This bribe succeeded, but not the controversy to include a dome on the renovated St Paul's, a neoclassical feature new to the authorities at St Paul's.

Then, in 1666, the Great Fire destroyed the old St Paul's and Sancroft did not hesitate to commission Wren to design its replacement, which he did, dome and all. But work did not start, due to political wrangling, until 1675, and was completed in 1710. Meanwhile, he completed the rebuilding of the fifty-three city churches, all in various shades of the neoclassical style.

Wren's third and final project in Cambridge was at Trinity College, the eponymous library which he modelled on that of St Mark's in Venice.

It measures two hundred feet long, forty-two feet wide and thirty-seven feet high. The bookcases were made by Grinling Gibbons and contain many treasured possessions, such as manuscripts of Milton's *Paradise Lost*, Tennyson's *In Memoriam* and Isaac Newton's private library. At the end of the bookcases are Wren's pedestals supporting busts of Trinity's famous alumni. The Library was completed in 1695.

A design sometimes attributed to Christopher Wren is the so- called Wren Bridge at St John's College Cambridge. Although he submitted a design, it was never used. Instead, Robert Grumbold was engaged to build the bridge as he was working upriver rebuilding Clare

College Old Court and its much admired bridge. Trinity's bridge is more correctly known, rather prosaically, as the Kitchen Bridge.

However, nobody can deny that Cambridge contains Christopher Wren's very first building design: Pembroke College Chapel.

THE THREE-MILE RULE (1702)

In order to be awarded their degrees, undergraduate students at Cambridge must live within the university's precincts during term time. In the case of Cambridge, this is three miles from Great St Mary's Church, which is situated in the centre of the city at the north end of King's Parade. For graduate students, the precincts are ten miles. In Oxford, the precincts for undergraduates are twenty-five miles. The origins of the three-mile rule are shrouded by the mists of time.

Interestingly, Girton College only just complies with the three-mile rule, being 2.9 miles from Great St Mary's.

Girton was the first female college in either of the two old universities when it was founded in 1869. The reason for it being so far from the centre of Cambridge was to discourage male students from other colleges visiting!

Great St Mary's Church is the university church and is one of the original Greater Churches network, of which there were fifty-five dotted around England. These churches were cathedral-like by virtue of their size, antiquity and ecclesiastical importance. At the same time, it is a parish church within the Diocese of Ely.

St Mary the Great was built in 1205 but the original structure was destroyed by a fire in 1290 and rebuilt. The present structure was completed in 1519 and played an important role in the life of the university. It was the official gathering place for meetings and debates, but this ceased in 1730 when the university's Senate House was built.

The patronage of Great St Mary's and the right to name the incumbent passed from the Crown to King's Hall in 1342. This in turn passed to Trinity, when King's Hall was taken over by Henry VIII's new creation, Trinity College in 1546. Since that date, the patronage of Great St Mary's has been with Trinity College.

Six of the eight university sermons are delivered at Great St Mary's each year, but it is no longer the centre of university ceremonials, such as the degree deremony. This has passed across the road to the Senate House. But the reference point for the university precincts and the three-mile rule is still the bell tower of Great St Mary's.

THE FIRST PRIME MINISTER (1721)

A favourite pub quiz question, and a recurring one in the English citizenship test for foreign-born nationals, is who was Britain's first prime minister? Well, as everyone knows, it was Robert Walpole in 1721.

Sir Robert Walpole, first Earl of Orford (1676–1745), was born at Houghton in Norfolk, the son of another Robert Walpole, a prominent Norfolk landowner and MP "owner" of the pocket borough of Castle Rising.

Young Robert Walpole was educated at Eton, before going on to King's College Cambridge in April 1696, but his university education was cut short by the death of his eldest brother in 1698. Walpole returned home to Houghton, now the heir, to learn how to manage the family estates. He married Catherine Shorter, the daughter of a wealthy timber merchant, soon after his return.

His father died in 1700, so young Robert duly inherited the constituency of Castle Rising, giving him a flying start to his political career. At the general election of 1702, he secured the seat at King's Lynn.

In fact, despite the nepotism, he proved to be an extremely capable and astute politician, and was a member of the fledgling, reforming Whig party (today's Liberal Democrats) who first came to power in 1715 at the expense of the Tories, and were to remain in power until 1760. The so-called Whig oligarchy.

Robert Walpole's rise was swift. In the Tory/Whig coalition of 1707–1710, he became Secretary at War in 1708, and Treasurer of the Navy in 1710. Then disaster briefly struck when he was expelled from the House and sent to the Tower of London for alleged corruption in the trial of the hard-line Anglican preacher Henry Sacheverell, who in his preaching fiercely attacked the Whig party. Although he was found guilty, his sentence was light, and because of his popularity with the masses he became a martyr, and enabled the Tories to come to power in 1710.

However, the accession of the Hanoverian George I to the throne in 1714 returned the Whigs to power in 1715. Walpole was released from the Tower and was appointed a Privy Councillor to George I. He was a very capable and able administrator and was, in 1715, appointed to the highest office in government: Chancellor of the Exchequer and First Lord of the Treasury.

By 1721, it soon became apparent that any governing party needed a leader to control and decide on a common path in the face of the contrary views within government. And thus came into being the supreme post of prime minister. Robert Walpole possessed all of the political and organisational skills necessary and he retained the position until 1742. Over twenty years, the longest-serving UK prime minister in history.

What is so amazing is that he continued to serve for the whole of this period, 1721–1742, as Chancellor of the Exchequer and First Lord of the Admiralty as well. After his tenure, the roles were separated, but the prime minister retains the nomenclature First Lord of the Treasury in the title.

Since Walpole's time, there have been fifty-six prime ministers, fourteen of whom have been educated at Cambridge University.

PEPYS' DIARY – A CODEBREAKER'S NIGHTMARE (1724)

In 1654, Samuel Pepys graduated from Magdalene College Cambridge, and by the end of the century, he was a very high-profile man of public affairs. He was a Member of Parliament, president of the Royal Society, but above all Secretary to the Admiralty.

It was in this latter post that he made his most important contribution: the creation of a professional Royal Navy, which was to become the largest navy in the world for nearly 250 years, covering the entire known world and underpinning the British Empire: "Rule Britannia".

Pepys was well-connected with the great and the good from Charles II downwards, and that is what makes his diaries so fascinating and his greatest legacy.

He lived in most interesting times: Charles II's Renaissance Britain, the Plague, the Great Fire of London and the Dutch Wars. Because his diaries were written in a little-known version of shorthand (Skelton's tachygraphy), they were quite indiscreet at times, especially his own peccadilloes with the opposite sex.

The diaries covered a period of nine years and five months, from 1st January 1660 to 31st May 1669, and ran to six volumes. They are more than one-and-a-quarter million words long and one-and-a-half times as long as the Bible.

They are Magdalene College's most prized possession and came to it with the rest of Pepys' library, as the result of two codicils to Pepys' will, dated 12th and 13th May 1603, just two weeks before he died.

His library consisted of 3,000 volumes, including Ovid's Roman works, a handwritten Wycliffe Bible, Newton's *Principia Mathematica* and Sir Francis Drake's nautical almanac.

The library was left in the first instance to his nephew John Jackson, who was charged with sorting it out into the precise order which Pepys had laid out in his will. On Jackson's death, the library was, as laid down in the second codicil, to pass to Magdalene College which it duly did in 1724. It is housed in the beautiful Pepys Building.

When first constructed in the late 17th century, the Pepys Building was known simply as "the new building", to which Pepys had contributed financially during his lifetime and into which, as laid down by his will and two codicils, his library should be housed in a room above the loggia. Gradually, the new building became known as the Pepys Building and the central arch bears the inscription

"Bibliotheca Pepysiana 1724". It is one of Cambridge's loveliest buildings.

However, it would not be for another 100 years after the diaries arrived at Magdalene that the contents would be deciphered. Pepys, as has been said, wrote them in a system of early shorthand known as tachygraphy (Greek for fast writing) which was quickly superseded by other shorthand forms and the Skelton system was lost in the mist of time.

So, in 1840, Magdalene persuaded a St John's graduate, the Reverend John Smith, to attempt to decipher Pepys' diaries. This turned out to be an extremely laborious job. He was aided by a short section which Pepys himself had translated.

Smith had almost finished when he found in Pepys' library, Skelton's 1647 instruction book. One can only imagine Smith's reaction! However, legal restrictions placed an embargo on publishing the juiciest bits, until 1979 when a complete and unabridged version was produced by an American, Professor William Matthew, an expert in the tachygraphy shorthand system, and Robert Latham, an authority in the history of the period. What we have is one of the most vivid accounts in the whole of English history of a specific decade.

THE CAMBRIDGE DON WHO HELPED ELECTRIFY THE WORLD (1729)

There lies on the summit of the North Downs above Charing in Kent amidst the rich foliage and majestic beech trees of its 200-acre park, Otterden Place, the seat of the Wheler family. It was purchased by Granville Wheler (1701–1770) in 1717, who was at the time an undergraduate of Christ's College Cambridge; he was later to become a fellow at Christ's.

It was in this idyllic setting that, on July 2nd 1729, a series of experiments was carried out that was to change the whole civilised world: the harnessing, by conduction, of the power of electricity.

The experiments were carried out by Stephen Gray (1666–1736) and his host, Granville Wheler, who was, with Gray, an early pioneer in the field of electrical conduction.

At the time of his experiments, Gray was a sixty-three-year-old retired silk dyer from Canterbury in Kent, who became an amateur astronomer of some distinction and who was also delving into the mysteries of electrical conduction. He was educated at one of the basic elementary schools that were springing up in the mid 17th century. He was an autodidact (self-taught) scientist who, in his youth, was so proficient that he came to the attention of John Flamsteed, the Astronomer Royal, who took him under his wing and nurtured his latent talent. Gray assisted Flamsteed, a member of Jesus College Cambridge, in setting up the Greenwich Observatory.

Gray then went to Cambridge to assist in the setting-up of an observatory. There, he began to delve into the mysteries of static electricity, which had been known about since the time of the Greek philosopher Plato, and until 1729 had been largely used as a phenomenon for public entertainment in theatres, coffee houses and at society weddings.

Granville Wheler was only twenty-eight when his ground-breaking experiments with Gray took place. He was fortunate in being at Cambridge in the wake of Sir Isaac Newton (Trinity), which heralded the dawning of a new age in which the teaching of mathematics and physical sciences was properly recognised.

Until the mid 17th century, Cambridge lagged behind Oxford, where the Savilian Professorships of Geometry and Astronomy were founded in 1619. The Royal Society, founded in 1662, consisted at first almost exclusively of Oxford men, Lord Brouncker and Christopher Wren amongst them. The problem was that Cambridge, until the mid 17th century, was exclusively devoted to the study of divinity and the classics, but the rest of Europe had recognised the importance of mathematics and physical sciences in a fast-changing world.

When Cambridge at last recognised the new studies, they took strong and immediate hold. The Lucasian Professorship of Mathematics was founded in 1664, and the Professorships of Astronomy in 1707 and Chemistry in 1703. It is fair to say that with the impetus given by Sir Isaac Newton, Cambridge never looked back and has dominated the field of physical sciences for the last 300 years.

Granville Wheler was a major beneficiary of this transformation and his college, Christ's, was at the forefront of the teaching of mathematics during this time, with one of its fellows chosen as the fourth Lucasian Professor of Mathematics in 1711, a post he held until 1739. This coincided with Granville Wheler's time at Christ's (1717–1724) so he had a good grounding in mathematics, graduating with a BA in 1721. He became a fellow in 1722 and proceeded to an MA in 1734.

On leaving university in 1734, he began delving into the mysteries of electricity and developed friendships with other pioneers in this intriguing field, particularly electrical conduction. Thus it was that Wheler invited Stephen Gray to Otterden Place to conduct experiments into electrical conduction.

Gray and Wheler realised that a bit of show business was required to draw attention to their ground-breaking experiments in the conduction of electricity, so an eight-year-old boot boy employed at Otterden was suspended in mid-air by silk threads which acted as insulators, so that they could pass the static electricity from a jar through the boy from his toes to his hands (conduction). A volunteer touched the boy's hands and received a shock which produced a dramatic spark for all the bystanders to see. Thus was born electrical conduction. Gray and Wheler went on to transmit electricity over a distance of more than 800 feet across the grounds of Otterden Park.

Both pioneers were appointed to the Royal Society. They had given future generations one of the greatest inventions the world has ever known. They had harnessed electricity so that it could be used in communications, lighting, power and air conditioning, both industrial and domestic. And it would soon replace the internal combustion engine to power motor vehicles.

FISRT EXPERIMENTS IN ELECTRICAL CONDUCTION

THE IRON BAR MYSTERY (1750)

One of Cambridge's unsolved mysteries concerns the rather prosaic iron bars that cut across the corners either side of the entrance towers to Christ's College and St John's College.

The iron bars are not things of great beauty; that's why they have gone unremarked and therefore are a mystery.

Numerous authorities have been consulted: the college porters, college archivists, domestic bursars, the Cambridge Archaeological Society and Cambridge Blue Badge Guides. None of them had a definitive answer.

Various uses have been suggested, such as a place where horses could be tied up or a means of preventing "peeping Toms" looking into college windows, and another, which seemed quite plausible, was to prevent potential muggers hiding in the dark corners of the entrance towers unnoticed, ready to pounce on people leaving the college.

Finally, it was suggested that the most revered authority on the architecture of England, Pevsner, should be consulted. His guide to Cambridgeshire contains the most detailed description of all the college buildings in Cambridge. Alas, no mention of iron bars. However, on contacting the author of Pevsner's Cambridgeshire, architectural historian Simon Bradley – bingo! – a definitive answer. To quote Mr Bradley verbatim, "My understanding is that iron bars of the kind shown in your photo were generally installed to prevent or reduce 'public nuisances', a euphemism for the use of such recesses and corners for urinating in. Undesirable at the best of times, and doubly so at the gates of an eminent Cambridge college."

Then came the question of when they were installed and for the answer to this question Simon Bradley referred me to the acknowledged authority on this sort of architectural detail, Charles Brooking, who opined that this type of iron bar construction and detail was probably late 18th or early 19th century.

THE IRON BAR MYSTERY

BRITAIN'S MOST LOVED POEM (1751)

"The curfew tolls the knell of parting day,
The lowering herd wind slowly o'er the lea,
The plowman homeward plods his weary way,
And leaves the world to darkness and to me."

This is the first verse of one of the most popular poems in the English language: Thomas Gray's "Elegy Written in a Country Churchyard" published in 1751.

Thomas Gray (1716–1771) was an English poet, historian, classical scholar and letter writer. A far cry from the career his family had planned for him as a lawyer. In fact, he even entered Peterhouse Cambridge with the intention of studying for a law degree.

Born in Cornhill, London on 26th December 1716, Thomas Gray was the fifth of twelve children born to Philip and Dorothy Gray and the only one to survive childhood. His father was a scrivener (scribe) mainly drawing up legal documents particularly those for loans. Dorothy, with her sister, had a millinery business.

Gray's mother paid for him to go to Eton College in 1725 where his uncles Robert and William Antrobus were tutors. He later recalled his schooldays as a time of great happiness as is evident in his "Ode on a Distant Prospect of Eton College" written in 1747. He made three close friends at Eton, Horace Walpole (son of Prime Minister Robert Walpole), Thomas Ashton and Richard West (whose father was Lord Chancellor of Ireland). They all shared an interest in poetry.

After Eton, Gray progressed onto Peterhouse Cambridge in 1734. This in itself is puzzling because King's College Cambridge was the usual destination for Eton pupils, being a twin foundation with Eton founded by Henry VI in 1440. Also, Trinity Hall was the specialist college for those wishing to study law. It was no wonder in letters to friends that he expressed dissatisfaction with the fellows at Peterhouse (sleepy, drunken and illiterate). As a result, he spent most of his time reading classical and modern literature.

After four years, he left Cambridge without a degree to embark on a Grand Tour of Europe with his friend from Eton, Horace Walpole. Italy and France were their destinations and Gray's blotting paper mind soaked up all that classical Europe had to offer plus the beautiful landscapes.

He returned from Europe in 1740 and lived with his parents until tragedy struck twice in 1741, with the death of his father and his great friend, Richard West. His father's wealth was all tied up in property and their Cornhill house was rented. His mother moved to Stoke Poges in Buckinghamshire to her sister's house. Gray, as a matter of financial expediency, moved back to Peterhouse where he could live quite cheaply and avail himself of the college's library, particularly the Greek section. He took and passed his law degree in 1743.

However, he did not practise law but remained at Peterhouse and pursued classical studies, self-taught, being one of the most brilliant minds of his day. A fellowship followed but more importantly, particularly after the death of Richard West, he began to devote more time to his poetry and in 1742 wrote "Ode on the Spring" and "On the Death of Richard West", which were well-received by the literary world. He also began what was to become his masterpiece, "Elegy Written in a Country Churchyard".

In 1747, Gray wrote "Ode to a Distant Prospect of Eton College", which again was a great critical success.

In 1749, his aunt, Mary, died, and he and his mother visited her grave in St Giles' churchyard in Stoke Poges on many occasions. This prompted him to finish his "Elegy Written in a Country Churchyard" which he did in 1750. He showed it to his friend Horace Walpole, who in turn showed it to his influential friends, who thought it quite brilliant. The pressure to publish became unstoppable and in 1751, Robert Dodsley published the poem to great critical acclaim. It was the making of Thomas Gray as a poet.

Amazingly, he only published thirteen poems but they were all masterpieces and contain more familiar phrases than any other group of poems in the English language. These include:

I. "Celestial fire"

II. "Far from the madding crowd" (used by Thomas Hardy for his 1874 novel)

III. "The paths of glory" (the title of a 1957 Stanley Kubrik film)

IV. "The unlettered muse"

V. "Kindred spirit"

VI. "'Tis folly to be wise"

In 1756, due to an unfortunate student prank, Gray moved across the road to Pembroke College, where he took up a fellowship.

In 1757, he was offered the prestigious post of Poet Laureate which he turned down. But in 1768, he accepted the Regis Chair of Modern History, a sinecure which carried a salary of £400 a year (about £20,000 a year in today's money).

Thomas Gray spent the rest of his life, until his death in 1771, studying early English and Celtic poetry and, when his duties allowed, travelling widely throughout Britain to places such as Yorkshire, Derbyshire, Scotland

and, most frequently, the Lake District. His love of nature and mountain landscapes was insatiable (this is graphically encapsulated in his journal of a visit to the Lake District in 1764).

He died in Cambridge in 1771, where he had spent most of his life, and was buried beside his mother and aunt in the churchyard of St Giles' church in Stoke Poges, the setting for his famous elegy.

THE GENTLEMEN CRICKETERS OF CAMBRIDGE (1755)

Although cricket had been played at Cambridge since the early 18th century, the first game of public note by a representative team of Cambridge University was advertised as a game between the Gentlemen of Cambridge University and the Gentlemen of Eton, which took place on 3rd July 1755, although the Cambridge University Cricket Club was not founded until 1820.

The first varsity match against Oxford took place in 1837 and was the first official sporting contest between England's two old universities; the first Boat Race followed in 1839.

In terms of international recognition, Cambridge University has produced twenty-one English Test captains out of a total of eighty since the first official Test match in 1877. Incidentally, Oxford University has produced thirteen. One of the reasons why Oxbridge, between them, have produced over 40% of Test captains was the requirement that only gentlemen (amateurs) and not paid players (professionals) could captain their country. The gentlemen either had private wealth or were employed in the professions (lawyers, doctors, accountants, etc.). Also, on the score card, gentlemen's initials preceded their surnames, i.e. M. J. K. Smith, and professionals after their surname, Titmus, F. J. The gentlemen also insisted on separate dressing rooms. It was a classic example of the English class system that prevailed until the 1950s, when in cricket at least it ceased in 1952 with the appointment of a working-class Yorkshireman, Len Hutton, as Test captain.

The distinction had manifested itself in an annual Gentlemen versus Players match at Lords. This anachronism ceased in 1962 when the last such match was played.

At least the six Cambridge educated cricketers who have captained England since 1954 have done so on merit, and include England's most successful captain of all time (on the basis of twenty or more games), Mike Brearley (St John's College), who out of a total of thirty-one games won eighteen matches, drew nine and lost only four.

GRAY'S ELEGIAC SOAKING (1756)

Arguably Britain's most popular poem was, for 200 years, Gray's "Elegy Written in a Country Churchyard".

Written by Thomas Gray (1716–1771) in 1751, whilst he was a fellow at Peterhouse Cambridge, it is the most celebrated of his thirteen published poems.

Gray spent the major part of his life at Cambridge, first as a fellow at Peterhouse, his alma mater, from 1725 until 1756, when, as the result of a student prank he moved across Trumpington Street to Pembroke College, where he was a fellow until his death in 1771.

The nature of the student prank to cause this upheaval was hilarious and could have come straight out of a Tom Sharpe novel.

Gray occupied rooms on the second floor of the Burrough's Building at Peterhouse. He had a dread of fire, partly due to what he considered to be the unruly and drunken behaviour of the undergraduates. So, to assuage his fears he ordered a thirty-four-foot rope ladder, which in the event of a fire he could attach to an iron bar, attached to the window sill. He could then climb his way down the thirty-four feet to the garden below.

One night in February 1756, students placed a water-filled barrel below Gray's window in the garden. They then stood on the stairs outside Gray's room and shouted, "Fire! Fire!" Gray opened his window and rapidly descended down his rope ladder and into the water-filled barrel. He was not amused and complained to the master, who, instead of being outraged, was as amused as the prank-playing students.

Gray promptly moved across the road to Pembroke where he considered the students more civilised, and where he would be accorded the respect due to Britain's most celebrated poet.

DOWNING'S OWN JARNDYCE
VERSUS JARNDYCE (1764)

Charles Dickens wrote *Bleak House* in 1852 to highlight the futility of long-contested probate cases. Jarndyce and Jarndyce, which featured in *Bleak House*, was such a case; it dragged on for nearly 100 years and, at the end of it all, the warring factions got not a penny.

What had started out as a fortune of the deceased, John Jarndyce who died without leaving a will, was totally eaten up in legal fees incurred by the contesting parties. Such cases were far from rare, which is why they are so loved by lawyers.

This work of fiction has much in common with the legal shenanigans which preceded the setting up of Downing College Cambridge in 1800.

In the Downing case, Sir George Downing (1685–1749) — the third baronet — did leave a will, whereby in the absence of an heir, he left the estate to a cousin, Jacob Garrard Downing. Although Jacob became the fourth baronet and initially inherited the Downing estate, he died without an heir in 1764. His cousin's will had provided for this eventuality: if Jacob died without an heir, the estate would go to three cousins in succession. If all four died without issue, the estate would be used to found a college at Cambridge, called Downing, although he himself did not attend Cambridge University. This last provision was almost an afterthought so unlikely were the chances of it coming to fruition, with at the time four male heirs standing first in line.

The second baronet, another Sir George Downing (1656–1711), the founder's father, and the fourth baronet, Sir Jacob Garrard Downing (1716–1764) had attended Cambridge University, Clare and Emmanuel College respectively, and Emanuel Downing (1585–1658), the father of the first baronet, had attended St John's College. The bulk of the Downing estate was created by the first baronet, Sir George Downing (1623–1684) through lucrative government appointments in the service of Oliver Cromwell and then Charles II, as has been explained in story eighteen earlier in this volume.

However, we return to Sir George Downing, the third baronet, and his will. At fifteen, he married his thirteen-year-old cousin Mary Forester, but the marriage was never consummated and a judicial separation took place. He did not marry again and so never produced a legal heir. He died in 1749 and the estates and baronetcy duly passed to his cousin Jacob, who became the fourth baronet; he died in 1764 without producing any legal heirs. In the meantime, to quote from Gilbert and Sullivan's *Mikado*, "by a set of curious chances" the other three named heirs had also died without producing any progeny.

At this point, Downing College should have come into existence, but Jacob's widow Margaret, who had not produced an heir, refused to give up the estate and there ensued a lengthy and costly legal battle, which was to last nearly forty years. Margaret had married again, so that when she died in 1778 her second husband carried on the fight on her behalf, assisted by a nephew.

Then, finally, the court decided in favour of Sir George's will, and Downing College was granted a Royal Charter. However, the costly legal battle and its ramifications had reduced the Downing estate to an estimated tenth of its original value in 1764.

As a result, the original design for the college was simplified in line with the reduced budget.

William Wilkins' original design was a unique campus-style college with buildings in the Grecian style. Initially only the West Range and part of the East Wing were completed, including the Master's Lodge, before the depleted funds ran out. The East Range was completed in 1873 when more funds were raised; further additions were made in the 20th century and piecemeal additions have been made in the 21st century.

However, the Downing campus with its wide lawns, is one of the most attractive colleges in Cambridge, even though the integrity of William Wilkins' original design was compromised in the 20th century when Sir Herbert Baker designed the North Range which now completes three sides of the court; the south side remains open. But nevertheless Wilkins' design predates Jefferson's University of Virginia campus-style by ten years, and therefore Downing is the oldest campus-style of any university in the world. However, unlike Dickens' Jarndyce versus Jarndyce battle, there were at least sufficient funds remaining to bring about Downing College's parturition.

Interestingly, the oldest part of Downing College did not transpire until 1960 when the foundation stone of the founder's childhood home, Dothill Park, Shropshire, was gifted to the college when that magnificent building was demolished. It bears the date 1628. Dothill Park was the home of his mother's sister Mary, who brought him up as her own when George's mother died when he was an infant. He was, in effect, adopted by Aunt Mary and grew up with her own daughter, another Mary. He had a happy childhood which he never forgot, so was very attached to Dothill Park and its vast estates. His own father was not considered fit to bring up a young child.

The big mistake was betrothing the two young children George and Mary, who were in effect brother and sister. And as recorded earlier, they were only fifteen and thirteen when they married. As has been said, the marriage was never consummated and the couple lived completely separate lives after George returned from his Grand Tour, and found that contrary to his wishes, she had accepted a lady in waiting position in the court of Queen Anne.

DOWNING COLLEGE CAMPUS DENUDED BY COSTLY LEGAL BATTLES.

Young Mary lived life at the court of Queen Anne. She attended one of the first race meetings held at Ascot in 1711. These meetings had been initiated by Queen Anne and were attended by Mary and, as a great beauty, she attracted much attention. It is said that it is Mary who initiated the custom of ladies wearing eye-catching and remarkable hats and, in turn, led to the advent of Ladies'

Day, a century later. It became known as Royal Ascot in 1768.

However, Mary and George obtained a legal separation but could not divorce, because the marriage was never consummated. As a result, Sir George, the third baronet, never married again and that, in effect, set in train the peculiar circumstances of the contested will.

THE AMERICAN FLAG AND THE WASHINGTON CONNECTION (1777)

Entering Cambridge from London along Trumpington Street, you pass on your left, first the Fitzwilliam Museum and then Cambridge's oldest college, Peterhouse (1284), and then just before Pembroke College's Wren Chapel on the right, you come to Little St Mary's Church (next door to Peterhouse).

American visitors usually make this little church a point of pilgrimage, because of its association with the family of Washington. The Reverend Godfrey Washington (1670–1729) was a fellow and bursar at Peterhouse and was appointed vicar of Little St Mary's in the early 18th century.

St Mary's had served as the Peterhouse Chapel until 1632 when the college built its own chapel.

When Godfrey Washington died in 1729, a memorial, in the form of a large tablet on the north wall of St Mary's, was installed which bears the Washington family coat of arms: a black eagle atop of a shield of red stars and stripes.

Godfrey Washington was the great-uncle of America's first president George Washington, and it was his family's coat of arms from which the stars and stripes of the United States national flag and US black eagle emblem are said to derive (1777).

The Washington family traces its roots to Sir William de Hertburn who was a descendent of the House of Dunkeld, descendants of Malcolm II of Scotland.

William the Conqueror granted William de Hertburn the manor of Wessyington in Durham. As was the fashion in those days, they adopted for their surnames the place where they were lords of the manor. Wessyington became Washington, and for 500 years or so the Washingtons were distinguished members of the County Durham landed gentry.

It was George Washington's great grandfather Colonel John Washington who first settled in the colony of Virginia in 1657, where he became a successful and wealthy tobacco planter and politician.

The rest is history, so to speak, and Cambridge has had connections with the United States for many years, particularly with Harvard University in Cambridge, Massachusetts and The Eagle Public House in Cambridge, England, but they are stories for another day.

Near this Place lyeth the Body of
the Late Rev.d Mr. GODFREY
WASHINGTON of the *County*
of *York. Minifter* of this Church
and *Fellow* of St. Peters Colledge
Born July the 26: 1670.
and Dyed the 28t. day of Sep.t
1729.

**THE WASHINGTON FAMILY COAT OF ARMS BASIS OF THE BASIS OF
THE AMERICAN FLAG "THE STARS AND STRIPES".**

THE MOST ROMANTIC BUILDING IN CAMBRIDGE (1831)

After the end of the Napoleonic Wars, Britain's economic prosperity increased and so did the demand for university education. Cambridge was no exception. St John's College between 1790 and 1859 grew from 120 to 370 students, and by the 1820s, the lack of space was becoming acute. If it was to expand, the college had to build on the western side of the River Cam because it possessed no more land to the east.

Despite its original intention to get the architects to build a copy of Second Court, the college eventually accepted a design in the romantic Gothic Revival style. The architects of this design were Thomas Rickman and Henry Hutchinson. They built what was, at the time, the largest single building erected by any college and did so in the face of considerable geotechnical problems. The land was marshy so large baulks of timber were laid down to form a raft on which the Ketton limestone structure would safely rest. The structure has held firm since its completion in 1831, although it was formidably expensive: £78,000, with an additional £44,000 for interest payments (in total equivalent to about £12 million today). The debt was finally cleared in 1857.

Named rather prosaically New Court, it is a romantic dream of late mediaeval style with pinnacles, cloisters and castellations abounding everywhere. It is crowned by a Gothic cupola containing a fan vault.

Connecting New Court on the western side of the River Cam with the main body of St John's College on the eastern side is the so-called "Bridge of Sighs", also designed by Henry Hutchinson. It is far prettier than its Venetian namesake. In fact, it more resembles the Rialto Bridge, also in Venice.

THE ST JOHNS WEDDING CAKE

New Court's prominent position (especially when viewed from the River Cam) and flamboyant design have led to it being nicknamed the "Wedding Cake". Nicholas Pevsner, the architectural historian, adored what he called the "fairy skyline".

QUEENS' MOVING APOSTROPHE (1831)

The Wars of the Roses (1455–1485), waged between the Houses of York and Lancaster, were ultimately settled by the coming to power of the son of Margaret Beaufort, a Lancastrian, Henry Tudor (Henry VII), who wisely married the daughter of the Yorkist monarch Edward IV, thus uniting the two warring families.

What is not generally realised is that Cambridge University, and particularly Queens' College, was a huge beneficiary of the successive queens thrown up by the fortunes of this terrible war, or to be more precise, series of wars.

First of all, in 1455 the incumbent ruler was the Lancastrian Henry VI, whose queen, Margaret of Anjou, in 1448 had founded Cambridge's Queen's College to complement her husband's foundation King's College, established in 1441.

In 1461, the Yorkist Edward IV deposed Henry VI at the Battle of Towton. However, Edward's wife Queen Elizabeth (Woodville) had been a lady in waiting at

Queen Margaret's court and was persuaded to take over the patronage of Queen's College.

On Edward IV's death in 1483, his Yorkist brother, the controversial Richard III, came to power and his wife Queen Anne (Neville) assumed the role of founder of Queen's. She settled lands on Queen's and the right to use Richard III's crest, the boar's head, as its second heraldic device.

Interestingly, the apostrophe in Queens' was not formally changed until 1831 from the singular Queen's to the plural Queens', thus linking forever the protagonists in the Wars of the Roses.

THE FITZWILLIAM MUSEUM – HOME TO THE WORKS OF JACK THE RIPPER? (1848)

As you enter Cambridge from the south along Trumpington Street, the first building of any note you encounter is the Palladian style Fitzwilliam Museum on the left.

Founded in 1816 under the terms of the will of Sir Richard Fitzwilliam Bart (1746–1816), the present building is the third to house his museum. From 1816 to1842, the museum was housed in the Perse School in Old School Lane, and from 1842 until 1848 the museum was housed in the Cambridge University Library.

Under the terms of Sir Richard's will, he provided £100,000 to be used to construct a museum to house his considerable library and extensive art collection.

The founder's building wasn't completed until 1848, hence the need for two temporary homes until the permanent home in Trumpington Street was completed.

Today, it contains the best collection of antiquities and modern art in western Europe. The treasures include art works by Monet, Rubens, Van Gogh, Rembrandt, Cezanne, Van Dyck and Canaletto.

It also contains no less than 187 paintings and drawings by Walter Sickert RA, RBA (1860–1942), one of Britain's most influential and controversial artists. He was the bridge between impressionism and modernism, changing the whole landscape of British painting.

Throughout his lifetime, he was outrageously controversial artistically, but the biggest controversy emerged thirty years after his death when he became a leading suspect for the Jack the Ripper murders.

Before proceeding further with the sensational suggestion that Sickert was Jack the Ripper, it is necessary to examine the life and times of this extraordinary extrovert.

It was odds-on that he was destined to be unconventional by the mere circumstances of his birth, in Munich in 1816. His father was the Danish-German artist Oswald Sickert and his mother Eleanor, English, the illegitimate daughter of astronomer Richard Sheepshank.

In 1868, the family moved to England as his father wished to avoid conscription to the German army. They settled in London where the young Walter Sickert received his education at King's College School.

On leaving school, he tried his hand as an actor with the Sir Henry Irving Company for a couple of years.

This, if nothing else, gave vent to a life-long desire to seek the limelight.

He then attended the Slade Art School but left after less than a year to become apprenticed to the flamboyant American artist James Whistler. As part of his training, he was sent on frequent missions to Paris where he met a whole range of contemporary French artists of the late 1860s. One in particular, Edgar Degas, had a great influence on him and helped him develop his own version of impressionism.

Whistler's flamboyance also rubbed off on him so controversy and experimentation did not daunt him.

He first came to the public's attention in the 1880s and he was invited to join the fledgling New English Arts Club in 1888, the bastion of figurative art, as opposed to the abstract form. It was seen as a sleeping stone to membership of the Royal Academy.

Sickert's first works to come to the attention of the public were scenes from the London music halls. One in particular, featuring the well-known music hall singer Katie Lawrence, was denounced by the critics as vulgar and tawdry, as female stage performers were seen as akin to prostitutes. But the public loved them. They represented an early manifestation of a recurring theme in his work: sexually provocative scenes.

Following his honeymoon in 1885, he spent much time in Dieppe for the rest of his life. It was a rich source of subject matter.

He also visited Venice and his portrayals of St Mark's Square are particularly memorable. And it was in Venice, in a period of inclement weather, that he started painting his sometimes sexually provocative nude scenes. His models were thought to have been prostitutes; probably clients. And it is with this work we can see the seeds of the "Jack the Ripper" theory. He further explored this theme on his return to London.

In 1911, Sickert formed the Camden Group of avant-garde British artists, and he even had a studio in this seamy part of London. His portrayal of the daily domestic scenes led to probably his most famous painting in this genre "Ennui" (1913).

His interest in the darker erotic nude scenes was further fuelled by the so-called Camden murder of 1907, where Emily Dimmock, a prostitute, after sexual intercourse had her throat cut. Sickert portrayed this murder with the evocative bedroom scene several times as the "Camden Town Murder" series. He took a great interest in the Jack the Ripper murders and even portrayed what he believed was Jack the Ripper's bedroom.

He was a particularly famous portrait painter whose subjects included George V, Lord Beaverbrook and Winston Churchill. He even gave the latter painting lessons, which prompted Churchill to write to his wife Clementine that Sickert had reawakened his interest in painting. Lord Beaverbrook had the largest collection of Sickert paintings in private hands.

It wasn't until the 1970s, over sixty years after the crime, that Stephen Knight in his book *Jack the Ripper: The Final Solution* set out to prove that Walter Sickert was the "Ripper". This accusation was largely based on information obtained from Sickert's illegitimate son Joseph Gorman, as well as the circumstantial evidence of his interest in Jack the Ripper. Gorman later admitted he had lied.

But the bandwagon had started to roll, with other writers examining the evidence and circumstances of Sickert's lugubrious interest in prostitutes, and his obsession with the Ripper.

The most compelling evidence was produced by the distinguished American crime novelist Patricia Cornwell, who wrote two books on the subject. Cornwell even purchased, at a cost of £6 million, thirty-one Sickert paintings in search of his DNA which she had compared with over 600 letters allegedly written by Sickert. She established that only one percent of the population had the same DNA. Scotland Yard poured scorn on her findings stating that the correct figure was 12.5 percent and that no court would convict on such inexact evidence, even with the circumstantial evidence which was just coincidence. Cornwell also suggested that Sickert was impotent due to a bodged operation on his genitals when a child. This, she claimed, made him extremely resentful of prostitutes who freely demonstrated their sexual prowess. Would a man, so sexually powerless, so obsessed with the female nude form in such erotic poses, be consistent with a male who was impotent? It would in many ways indicate the opposite: satyriasis, which in its extreme form could also cause what is known as a form of BDSM wishing to cause extreme pain as part of the sexual act.

It's an interesting theory and certainly consistent with Sickert's personality. Incidentally, Sickert died in Bath, Somerset in 1942 at the age of eighty-one. He had spent much time in the city in his later years and many of his paintings depict Bath's varied street scenes.

He had been married three times and produced no children; he may have been infertile rather than impotent although Joseph Gorman claimed to be his illegitimate son.

Whether the Fitzwilliam Museum in Cambridge is housing the works of so-called Jack the Ripper, self-professed killer of five women, is still an open question and certainly adds interest to a visit to the Fitzwilliam Museum.

ST CATHARINE'S - THE GREEK INFLUENCE (1860)

Cambridge graduate the late Colin Dexter (Christ's, 1953), creator of Morse and National Crossword Champion on six occasions, was clearly a man of words. He used to maintain that if you wanted to give a girl the most options for name interpretation, call her Catherine, e.g. Kate, Cathy, Katie, Kathryn, Catharine etc.

The fellows of St Catharine's in 1860 must have felt the same way, when they changed the name of their 1473 foundation from Katharine's Hall to St Catharine's College.

However, one would have thought that they were rather stuck with Catherine (with an e and not a second a) because the college had originally been named after St Catherine of Alexandria as evidenced by the college crest, a golden wheel, which sits on top of the entrance gate.

St Catherine of Alexandria was, in the 4th century, tortured for her Christian beliefs. The most notorious of her tortures consisted of being tied to the spoke of a large wheel with knives attached. The machine broke, so she was beheaded. The Catherine Wheel firework is named after her.

The Oxford Book of Saints lists three St Catherines but no St Catharine, but St Catherine of Alexandria of wheel fame is given an alternative spelling of St Katharyn.

The fellows, in 1860, used part of the alternative spelling, replacing the K with a C.

Various explanations are given for the change, including the need to differentiate it from St Catherine's Oxford. But that doesn't hold water, because the Oxford St Catherine's wasn't founded until 1962.

The most plausible explanation would seem to be it was named after the Greek word *catharus*, meaning pure or gentle, a characteristic they clearly wanted to emphasise at that time.

In England, her cult is widespread. Sixty-two churches are dedicated to her. There are murals in fifty-six churches as well as stained glass in York Minster, Oxford Cathedral and Balliol College Oxford. She is the patron saint of young girls, students, philosophers and craftsmen working with wheels.

CAMBRIDGE UNIVERSITY –
BIRTHPLACE OF THE "BEAUTIFUL GAME" (1863)

Association Football, or soccer for short, and now known simply as football, is the most popular sport in the world. It is played by 211 representative national teams who are members of the football world's governing body FIFA (Federation Internationale de Football Association).

However, the game in its present form was based on the Cambridge Rules which were first drawn up in a room in Trinity College in 1843 and modified in 1863, to become the founding rules of the Football Association founded in that same year.

What the Cambridge Rules effectively did was to separate the kicking game from the handling game, rugby, and the associated mayhem that went with it.

Soccer and Rugby Union effectively went their own ways, and it is due to the university footballers of Cambridge that we have this worldwide phenomenon known as the "beautiful game".

Initially the most successful teams were from the public schools, Eton, Charterhouse, Harrow (named the Wanderers), and the universities of Oxford and Cambridge, plus the Royal Engineers representing the British Army.

When the FA Cup was introduced in 1872, it was one of these elite clubs who won the competition for the first ten years.

It was only after the introduction of professional football that the dynamic of the game changed from a game exclusively played by gentlemen to the working man's game, and we have Blackburn Rovers to thank, for they won the FA Cup four years running from 1884.

Thereafter it was only the professional teams from the Midlands and North of England that won the FA Cup until 1901, when Tottenham Hotspur won the cup, beating Sheffield United 2–1 in front of a record crowd of 110,820 at Crystal Palace.

The world's first international match took place between England and Scotland in 1872 in Glasgow; it ended in a 0–0 draw. England was captained by an Oxford undergraduate, Cuthbert Ottaway. Cambridge had one player in the team, John Brockbank.

Cambridge University was a founder member of the FA governing body, along with Oxford University, and is still a member to this day, and Cambridge University FC is recognised as the oldest football club in the world.

THE GATE OF NECESSITY FOR THOSE IN NEED (1868)

John Lennon, in The Beatles' film *A Hard Day's Night*, famously remarked that Ringo Starr's drums "loom large in his legend". The same may be said of the Gates of Gonville and Caius, Cambridge's fourth oldest college, founded in 1348.

Officially there are four gates: the Great Gate, which is the entrance to the college by the Porters' Lodge, and then three other gates which reflect the students' progress through the college during different stages of their academic life.

They are, in chronological order: the Gate of Humility through which the fresher students pass upon matriculation at the start of their studies; the Gate of Virtue through which they pass throughout their studies; and, lastly, the magnificent Gate of Honour.

The Gate of Honour is, by far, the most prestigious, with its hexagonal top embellished by six sundials. It is through this gate that a student passes from Caius Court to the university's Senate building, just a few yards away across Senate Passage, to receive their degree upon graduation.

However, there is one further unofficial gate which the students have themselves created, the Gate of Necessity, connecting Tree Court to Gonville Court, which contains some lavatories, providing urgent relief for those students returning from a liquid night out, particularly at the end of term.

MURDER MOST FOUL – REVENGE FOR A SHILLING (1876)

On Thursday night, 24th August 1876, there took place on the Butt's Green area of Midsummer Common probably Cambridge's most gruesome murder. The victim, a fifteen-year-old child prostitute by the name of Emma Rolfe, was all but decapitated by twenty-five-year-old tailor's assistant, Robert Browning. He had recently been discharged from the army on mental health grounds and had recently spent a spell in the Addenbrooke's Hospital being treated for advanced venereal disease (syphilis).

The murder was a premeditated revenge murder; the victim merely being representative of the profession which had inflicted the terrible disease on the clearly culpable victim. He was a frequent customer of prostitutes and one in particular, who he reckoned was responsible for his present condition. However, she was not the victim; one of her profession, the unfortunate Emma Rolfe, happened to be in the right place at the wrong time.

Robert Browning, with his brother, had finished a tailoring job that day, for which they had been paid an extra five shillings for finishing on time. So, he was feeling flush and after a courage-boosting drink with his brother at The Cranham Arms in Field Street, he met Emma Rolfe in the infamous "red light" district of Cambridge's Four Lamps at the end of Maids Causeway, which fronts Midsummer Common. In fact, he met two prostitutes, Emma and one other whom he rejected. He then took Emma to the adjacent Butt's Green where a furious argument first took place about the paltry shilling she required for her services (equivalent to about £5 in today's money). Once they had ceased arguing, without further ado, he produced a cut-throat razor and cut her throat with such force that her head was almost separated from her body.

Browning left the victim where she fell and, covered in blood, he paid a call to The Garrick inn on the corner of King Street and Jesus Street at the Four Lamps intersection. He ordered half a pint of beer while he contemplated his next move.

Meanwhile, Emma's screams had alerted Joseph Wheeler, a policeman who had been patrolling the area, and as he passed The Garrick, Browning emerged and immediately confessed to having murdered a girl on Butt's Green. He then took the somewhat sceptical PC Wheeler to the scene of the crime, accompanied by a passerby. The scene that greeted them was horrific, as might be imagined. Robert Browning was taken to the nearest police station where he was formally charged with murder.

Browning was detained in Norwich Jail to await the November Assizes in that city. He was duly tried and found guilty. However, during the course of the trial, a history of mental illness was found to be present in the male line of the Browning family and the jury recommended that on the grounds of his youth and mental condition, clemency should be extended to Browning when sentencing him.

The Home Office, after considering reports from the Inspector of Prisons, upheld the death sentence.

Shortly after 8 a.m. on 15th December 1876, Browning was led to the gallows and duly hanged. He was the first person to be executed within the walls of Cambridge Gaol.

The Garrick has since been demolished and replaced by a hostelry named St Radegund, named after St Radegund, a saint associated with Jesus College.

THE CAMBRIDGE FOOTLIGHTS: A COMEDIC REVOLUTION (1883)

The Cambridge University Footlights Dramatic Club, commonly referred to simply as the "Footlights", was formed in 1883 as an alternative to the exclusive Cambridge University Amateur Dramatic Club (ADC), founded in 1851, whose membership was restricted to members of Trinity College. The Footlights was open to all Cambridge University college members.

The ADC originally met in rooms rented from the Hoop Lane Inn, Jesus Lane. However, it was not long before its wealthy Trinity College members were able to purchase, in 1882, its present freehold premises in Park Street.

The university authorities did not approve, as they thought it would distract students from their studies, particularly drama. In the words of one Magdalene don, "Gentlemen don't act." However, when Trinity alumnus Edward VII became honorary president, attitudes softened.

The Footlights used to meet in rooms in The Falcon Inn, until city centre redevelopment forced them to move in with the ADC in the 1970s.

Not long after its foundation, the Footlights changed its emphasis to comedy, and each year produced a revue which appeared every May Week at the Theatre Royal, Cambridge and then went on to the Edinburgh Festival Fringe after the latter's foundation in 1947. In truth it was no more than an "end of pier concert party" and it trundled along in this mode for the next eighty years.

Then, in the late 1950s and early 1960s, a unique intake of students transformed the Footlights. This was the catalyst for the "satire boom" with its production of *The Last Laugh* written by Peter Cook, featuring not only Cook but also Eleanor Bron. Then came a joint production with the Oxford University Revue, *Beyond the Fringe*, featuring Peter Cook and Jonathan Miller from the Footlights, and Dudley Moore and Alan Bennett from the Oxford Revue. Such was its international success that the Footlights became a national institution. The "satire boom" and its creators are the subject of another story in this volume.

Hard on the heels of the *Beyond the Fringe* team followed John Cleese, Bill Oddie and Tim Brooke-Taylor who, in 1963, wrote and performed *Cambridge Circus*, which transferred to the New Arts Theatre Club in London, where it received favourable critical reviews and as a result toured New Zealand.

The radio series "I'm Sorry I'll Read that Again" was created by the *Cambridge Circus* team in 1964. It spawned *The Goodies* in 1970 in which Tim Brook-Taylor, Graeme Garden and Bill Oddie appeared and *I'm Sorry I Haven't a Clue* in 1972, in which Tim Brook-Taylor appeared until his death in 2020.

John Cleese has the distinction of appearing in some of the most popular television series ever, including *Monty Python's Flying Circus* (1964 to 1974) which spawned five Monty Python films, most notably *The Life of Brian* in 1979. However, he will be forever remembered for his role as the dysfunctional Basil Fawlty in *Fawlty Towers*, which he co-wrote and starred with his then wife Connie Booth. It ran for two series in 1975 and 1979, and in 2019 was named greatest ever British TV sitcom by a panel of comedy experts assembled by the Radio Times. His most notable film is probably *A Fish Called Wanda* in which he starred with Jamie Lee Curtis, Kevin Kline and Michael Palin. At the age of eighty-one, he still continues to work, he maintains, to pay the maintenance arising from three divorces.

The next notable explosion of talent in the Footlights was in the 1980s when the Footlights 1981 revue appeared at the Edinburgh Fringe Festival, starring Emma Thompson, Hugh Laurie, Stephen Fry and Tony Slattery, and spawned *A Bit of Fry and Laurie*, a television series which ran from 1987 to 1995.

They have appeared in numerous other projects, most notably *Jeeves and Wooster* (1990–1993). Hugh Laurie then decamped to America where he starred in *House*, an American television drama from 2004–2012. He was one of the highest-paid actors in a television drama, earning £250,000 per episode. He also received two Golden Globe awards.

Stephen Fry has made numerous film appearances, most notably starring as Oscar Wilde in *Wilde* in 1997. He has also written four novels and three autobiographies. Fry and Laurie also appeared with Rowan Atkinson in the *Blackadder* series, shown from 1983–1989.

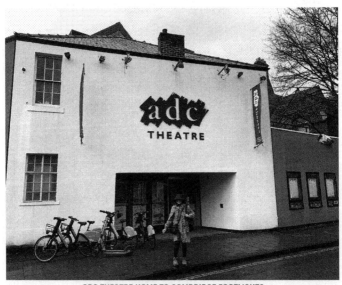

ADC THEATRE HOME TO CAMBRIDGE FOOTLIGHTS

Dame Emma Thompson is one of Britain's most acclaimed actresses, the recipient of two Academy Awards, three BAFTAS and two Golden Globes. Her early successes include *Howard's End*, *The Remains of the Day* and *Sense and Sensibility*.

The Footlights home is the ADC Theatre in Park Street, off Jesus Lane, and it continues to appear at other venues as the ADC only seats 100, so every May week they perform at Cambridge's larger Theatre Royal and, of course, every August at the Edinburgh Festival Fringe. It continues to maintain a steady flow of comedic talent, but it will be forever remembered for its crucial role in the 1960s "satire boom".

HM POSTMASTER GENERAL
BANS COLLEGE STAMPS (1886)

Oxbridge colleges had always used a messenger service for delivering letters locally. However, the bookkeeping involved was horrendous as the charges for delivery had to be entered on the sender's account for board and lodging and other expenses (known as battels in some colleges).

In order to save the cost of entering such trivial amounts, eight colleges in Oxford and Cambridge started to adopt a system of prepayment by issuing their own postage stamps for use for deliveries within Oxford and Cambridge.

Keble College Oxford was the first to issue its own stamps in 1871, to be followed by seven other Oxford colleges and three Cambridge colleges: Selwyn (1882), Queens' (1883) and St John's (1884). The stamps all bore the names of their colleges and were much used, especially when used in conjunction with specially designed college stationery.

Fearing the system might spread, the Postmaster General (PMG), on 28th January 1886, announced he was banning the use of college stamps, on the grounds that the system was an infringement of the Post Office monopoly. Fortunately, the PMG was a graduate of Trinity College Cambridge so no offence was caused by his own alma mater.

By way of compensation and to prove it could provide a comparable service, the Post Office installed red postboxes outside the main entrance of most colleges and announced an improved collection and delivery service. Three collections and deliveries a day, seven days a week.

Today, the stamps are much sought after by philatelists.

FOSTERS' BANK - TRUE VICTORIAN SPLENDOUR (1891)

The Foster brothers, Ebenezer (1776–1851) and Richard (1787–1859), and their direct descendants, Charles and Henry, were pillars of Cambridge society of the town variety. They founded three flour mills in the centre of Cambridge in the late 18th century and, more audaciously, Fosters' Bank in 1804. This was more as a convenience for their employees.

At this time, banks were springing up all over the provinces and many failed. Fosters' Bank was not one of the lame ducks. It was, on the other hand, a huge success, spawning ten branches all over East Anglia.

The head office was for many years in Trinity Street, Cambridge.

The wealth generated by the flour milling and bank businesses allowed them to be benefactors to many good causes, most notable Addenbrooke's Hospital of which Ebenezer was a very hands-on governor. They also fulfilled their civic duties, by serving on Cambridge District Council as aldermen, mayors and high sheriffs of the county.

By the end of the 19th century, with typical Victorian hubris, they built a huge mill next to the railway station which was capped by a castellated tower. Quite the largest commercial building in Cambridge.

However, their lasting legacy was the building of a new head office at Fosters' Bank in 1891. As a result of the bank's great success, they outgrew their quaint head office in Trinity Street. With typical Victorian self-confidence, they found a site in Sidney Street on the corner with Hobson Street, and commissioned Britain's leading architect, Alfred Waterhouse, to build a bank which would be the grandest in the whole of East Anglia. Waterhouse had recently built Manchester Town Hall, the Natural History Museum in London, and many college buildings both in Oxford and Cambridge. He didn't come cheap but money was no object as far as the Fosters were concerned.

The Waterhouse design for the Fosters' new flagship was a wonderful example of neoclassical Gothic which was a Waterhouse specialty. The building was constructed of ashlar limestone with bands of red brick surmounted by an octagonal ornate clock and spire. Above the entrance was proudly displayed the proud appellation "Fosters' Bank".

The exterior is a sight to behold, matching in grandeur the university architecture for which Cambridge is famous. But, like King's College, it is difficult to decide whether it is the exterior or the interior which takes precedence. In Fosters' case, the interior is breath-taking, with its huge domed banking hall ornately tiled in true Victorian splendour. The mahogany serving counters and rails complete a truly stunning architectural gem. It is matched by only one other working banking hall in Britain and that is the Royal Bank of Scotland banking hall in Edinburgh.

The Foster brothers' two traditional businesses are no longer owned by the family. As is the way with these things, small is no longer beautiful. Their milling operation was acquired by Spillers and Rank Hovis, whilst their banking operation was taken over by Lloyds in 1919.

However, the Victorian bank building is one of Cambridge's must-see attractions, particularly the banking hall.

THE TWO LADY ADVENTURERS
WHO FOUND THE HIDDEN GOSPELS (1892)

In 1892, two Cambridge-based twin sisters, Agnes Smith Lewis (1843–1929) and Margaret Dunlop Gibson (1843–1920), née Agnes and Margaret Smith (sometimes referred to as the Westminster Sisters or the Heavenly Twins), caused a sensation when at St Catherine's Monastery on Mount Sinai they unearthed one of the earliest translations of the Bible, the so-called 4th century *Syriac Sinaiticus*.

Against all the odds, they undertook the arduous journey to Mount Sinai by primitive boat, camel and on foot until they reached St Catherine's Monastery. By dint of their fluency in modern Greek, they enchanted the brethren and overcame the natural hostility towards women and were allowed to examine the manuscripts containing the four canonical gospels of the New Testament: Matthew, Mark, Luke and John.

Their visit followed the ground-breaking discovery forty years earlier by a German scholar, Constantin von

Tischendorf, of the *Codex Sinaiticus*, a biblical manuscript also from the 4th century.

Together, the two discoveries provided a timely confirmation of the contents of the Bible at a time when its accuracy was being questioned on the basis that, over the centuries, the "message" may have been distorted, a bit like "Chinese whispers". So, the two discoveries provided an opportunity to check the Bible's accuracy.

Altogether, the sisters learnt more than twelve languages between them, including most European languages as well as the biblical languages of Hebrew, Ancient Greek and Syriac. So, who were these two remarkable women?

Margaret and Agnes Smith were born in Irvine, North Ayrshire in Scotland in 1843, to a prosperous Scottish lawyer, John Smith, and his wife Margaret who died shortly after giving birth. Their father, who was an amateur linguist, brought his daughters up as though they were sons and imbued in his daughters his own facility with languages, on the understanding that once mastered they would visit the country concerned. So, they became much travelled. Sadly, their father died when they were only twenty-two.

After their father's death, they did a lot of travelling abroad, including Jerusalem and Cairo, before moving permanently to London in 1869, followed by studies in Greek and Arabic and trips to Greece.

Both sisters married, Margaret to a former Presbyterian minister, James Gibson, in 1883, who sadly died three years later.

The sisters' next trip was to Cambridge to enjoy the splendours of the architecture and to engage in intellectual discourse with the academics. One in particular, Samuel Lewis, the librarian at the Parker Library, Corpus Christi, was an antiquarian and dedicated traveller. Agnes had met her perfect match and nine months later, they were married. They built a magnificent residence, Castlebrae, on Castle Hill, Cambridge. It became a focal point for intellectual discussion and the sisters made an enormous impact with their knowledge of the Holy Land and biblical languages, so much so that they became known as the "Heavenly Twins". But Agnes' marriage, like her sister's, lasted only three years before Samuel Lewis succumbed to a heart attack.

Then, in 1882, they received a tip-off from James Randall Harris, a biblical scholar and fellow at Clare College, who had recently returned from a visit to St Catherine's Monastery. He had discovered some old manuscripts locked away in a chest; although they looked interesting, he didn't have time to examine them properly.

In 1892, the twins, armed with letters of introduction from Randall Harris and the university vice-chancellor, made their arduous journey to St Catherine's and as explained, greatly impressed the brotherhood, who let them examine the 179 folios which were palimpsests containing on the upper surface "Lives of female saints". Underneath were the gospels which were painstakingly revealed and photographed.

Arriving back in Cambridge with their evidence, they were initially treated with scepticism. After all, they were only women! However, on close examination, their male detractors had to admit that they "had something". An expedition was organised comprising the leading Cambridge authorities in the field of biblical studies: Professor Robert Bensly, Mr Francis Burkitt and, at the twins' insistence, Randall Harris and, of course, the twins. They also took Bensly's and Burkitt's wives along for propriety's sake.

They spent forty days at St Catherine's, painstakingly photographing and transcribing the gospels. When back in Cambridge, the University Press published the full transcript under the supervision of Agnes in October 1894.

The twins' reputation was firmly established and they received honorary degrees from the universities of Halle, Heidelberg, Dublin and St Andrews, but not Cambridge where degrees were not awarded to women until 1948.

This was just the beginning. The twins embarked on more expeditions and more projects using their unique understanding of the biblical languages.

However, they will always be known as the "Sisters of Sinai", which is the title of an excellent book by Janet Soskice which tells their remarkable story.

TWO LADIES WHO FOUND THE GOSPELS

BEWARE, WOMEN ON THE WARPATH (1897)

Women were not allowed a university education until 1869, with the founding of Girton College Cambridge, followed by Newnham College in 1871. The first female college in Oxford was Lady Margaret Hall in 1878. However, even though they took the same exams as men in both universities, they were not awarded degrees until 1920 at Oxford and 1948 at Cambridge.

Outrageous though this situation may seem from today's perspective, at the time when women were admitted to Oxford and Cambridge the most almighty furore was unleashed. It was as though the very basis of civilisation was being challenged: the natural order of things. Women's brains were not designed for such intellectual pursuits and they would have a disrupting effect on university life. They didn't look a bit like men!

The first major vote in Cambridge on the question of awarding women degrees took place in 1897 against scenes of great hysteria, resulting in a negative vote in the senate (the governing body of Cambridge University) of 1707 to 661. Nor were members of the senate alone in their apprehension. An undergraduate poll organised by The Cambridge Review produced an adverse vote of 1723 to 446. The anxiety of the young men, it is said, was over the prospect of effemination and the maintenance of sporting supremacy over Oxford. The uproar lasted for many weeks and was known as the "Women's War" and women were referred to as the Invaders.

It is instructive to record when degrees were awarded to women at other British universities: Britain's third oldest university, St Andrew's in Scotland, awarded degrees to women in 1895, London 1878 and Durham 1898.

When another vote was held in 1921, in the wake of Oxford's decision to admit women to degrees, a negative vote of 908 to 694 was recorded, and a rampaging mob went out to Newnham College and defaced its memorial gates.

It is appropriate to pause here to look at the social make-up of fellows and undergraduates at our great universities. They were products of the dysfunctional Victorian public schools so brilliantly portrayed in Alex Waugh's controversial novel *Loom of Youth*.

These "boys' own"-only institutions were totally sports orientated and females were viewed as if from another planet. But as the 20th century progressed, more state schoolboys entered Cambridge, who were perfectly used to the company of girls. In effect, two prejudices were being removed at the same time: class and sex!

Finally, in 1948, Cambridge women were awarded degrees and now the undergraduate population contains an equal number of males and females. Currently, fifteen heads of colleges are female, out of a total of fifty-one, and there have in recent years been two female university vice-chancellors.

THE JOY OF PUNTING (1902)

"Messing About on the River" is a popular song from the 1960s composed by Tony Hatch ("Downtown"), and describes perfectly the quintessential Cambridge tourist activity, punting.

Whether applied to self-hired or chauffeured punting, it is the quickest and most leisured way to view Cambridge University's most prestigious colleges: St John's, Trinity, Trinity Hall, Clare, King's and Queens'. And there is no danger of being mown down by Cambridge's ubiquitous bicycles, although the occasional self-hirer ends up in the river!

Cambridge is undoubtedly the punting centre of the United Kingdom but it was not always so, and leisure was not always its purpose.

A punt is a flat-bottomed boat with no keel and a square-cut bow, designed for use in small rivers or other shallow waters. The normal method of propulsion is by using a sixteen-foot long pole and literally pushing against the river bed. The pole is also used to steer, either as a tiller or a rudder. Hence the term "punting".

Punts were developed in mediaeval times as cargo boats for shallow parts of the River Thames and the fenlands north of Cambridge. But in the late 19th century, they became redundant, overtaken by more modern forms of transport such as the burgeoning railways.

Pleasure punts — specifically built for recreation — first appeared on the River Thames between 1860–1880. Cambridge followed in about 1902–1904 and they rapidly became the most numerous craft on the River Cam. Other locations, such as Oxford, Canterbury and Stratford, followed, but not with the same dominance.

The number of passengers a punt can carry is limited by the Coastguard Agency to twelve, because the Cam, for example, comes under the category of narrow rivers and canals, where the depth of the water is less than 1.5 metres.

The River Cam is particularly suited to punting due to a stone causeway being placed on the bed of the Cam by conservators, so as to allow horses drawing barges to wade up the middle of the river and avoid paying tolls to the Cambridge colleges for crossing their lands. The stone bed makes punting far easier and reduces the chance of the pole getting stuck in the silt.

A completely different scenic view from the classic colleges' trip, from the moorings opposite Magdalene College to Silver Street adjacent to Queens', can be had by crossing Silver Street and skirting the Mill pool and picking up a punt from Granta moorings. You then proceed in a southerly direction with meadows on either bank where you may picnic. The destination is the village of Grantchester, three miles distant, where the pleasures of an idyllic village await: three pubs and a tea room. The Red Lion and The Green Man are the pick of the three pubs whilst the Orchard Tea Gardens are legendary, being a particular favourite of the poet Rupert Brooke.

MAGDALENE PUNT HIRE STATION

The village of Grantchester has received national recognition by being featured in a detective series entitled *Grantchester*, starring Robson Green and James Norton. The city of Cambridge also provides a backcloth to this popular television series.

Finally, for something special, punting at night along the Backs by moonlight, with college lights glowing in the background makes for an unforgettable romantic journey, especially with a bottle of wine to hand.

Yes, "Messing About on the River" really does epitomise the joy of punting.

THE GHOST STORIES OF M. R. JAMES (1904)

Montague Rhodes James was born in 1862 near Sandwich in Kent, the son of a comfortably off rector but brought up in the Suffolk countryside. Although big and strong physically, he had no interest in games, preferring to spend hours in the local landowner's library.

When he arrived at Eton, he was pleasantly surprised to find the "bookish" were as welcome as the athletic. He won many prizes in the classics and found Eton and its close association with King's College Cambridge (they were twin foundations of Henry VI) congenial homes where he would spend the rest of his life as scholar, lecturer, dean, and provost at both foundations, and from 1913–1915 vice-chancellor of Cambridge University.

James was a mediaevalist scholar of international repute and wrote many scholarly works, many based on his worldwide excavations. He was also a dynamic director of the Fitzwilliam Museum at Cambridge and was responsible for securing many of its artefacts, not least notable portraits by Titian.

Given this formidable scholarly background, it comes as a great surprise to learn that Montague Rhodes James is none other than probably the greatest writer of ghost stories in the English language: M. R. James.

However, Cambridge was the seedbed for his earliest works. His Christmas Eve readings of his latest ghost stories to the Chit-Chat Society in the provost's parlour of King's College was the ideal setting. Candlelit, with a blazing fire, and with an easterly wind outside driving snow against the windows added to the sense of drama. In fact, it was a device used many years later when four of his stories were, on Christmas Eve 2000, broadcast on BBC Four read by the master of horror, Christopher Lee.

Radio and television adaptations of M. R. James' stories have appeared regularly since 1932; the latest, *The Mezzotint*, on Christmas Eve 2021 on BBC Two with a cast led by Rory Kinnear.

Altogether M. R. James wrote and published forty ghost stories spanning a period of over thirty years.

After thirty-six years at King's College, he returned, in 1918, to Eton College as provost, a position he occupied until his death in 1936. His whole life was spent in academe and he never married, although he had some close relationships with the opposite sex; he was asexual.

In his reading habits, he was a traditionalist. His favourite writers were Shakespeare, Dickens and he was a great fan of Agatha Christie. But the new wave of writers, such as Aldous Huxley, Lytton Strachey and James Joyce, he detested. He was, in the words of his great Cambridge friend A. C. Benson (the writer of the words to "Land of Hope and Glory"), an old-fashioned reactionary.

He was critically acclaimed by his peers. Sir John Betjeman, the poet, reckoned his ghost stories were the best he had ever read. Michael Sadleir (*Fanny by Gaslight*) described James as the best ghost story writer England has ever produced. Paul Theroux, the great American writer, described *The Mezzotint* as the most frightening story he had ever read.

James incorporated his antiquary background into his stories, which have become a genre of their own and with a great influence on other writers such as Kingsley Amis in his novel *The Green Man*, and today's great supernatural writers, including Stephen King. A large number of writers in the 20th century deliberately wrote in the Jamesian style, including Sir Arthur Gray, R. H. Malden (*Nine Ghost Stories*), L. T. C. Rott (*Sleep No More*) and A. N. L. Munby (*The Alabaster Hand*).

Although James conjures up strange beasts and supernatural manifestations, the shock effect of his stories is usually strongest when he is dealing with physical mutilation, because he believed that ghosts should be evil and repulsive, "more kindly ghosts belong in fairy tales".

An example of this philosophy can be found in *Lost Hearts*, where pubescent children are taken by a sinister dabbler in the occult who cuts out their hearts while they are still alive!

The final accolade was in 2012 when the Royal Mail released a stamp featuring James as part of its "Britons of Distinction" series.

If you haven't read a James ghost story then you should, if you dare and are of a strong mental constitution.

THE MYSTERY OF THE CHRIST'S COLLEGE GHOST (1918)

It is not often, if ever, a ghost gets the chance to explain itself and give an indication as to why its troubled soul can't rest in peace.

However, the ghost of so-called Christopher Round at Christ's College is given that chance in a fifty-six-page monograph by a resident history don by the name of A. P. Baker, published by Heffers in 1918.

With the passing of over 100 years, opinions have become the subject of much conjecture. How much of A. P. Baker's account is true and how many of the participants are figments of Baker's imagination?

What is not in dispute is that from the mid 19th century, an apparition has regularly been sighted in the Fellows' Garden by quite unconnected scholars, dons and college guests; and the date of the sighting is always the same: 29th May.

Their description of the apparition bears a remarkable and detailed resemblance. A tall figure of advanced years dressed in a swallowtail coat, fashionable in the mid 19th century. The figure would emerge onto the Fellows' Garden lawn from under the chestnut trees on the left as observed from the Fellows' Building, and walk slowly and deliberately with head bent as far as the great yew and the weeping ash. He then turns off and disappears before reaching the Malcolm Bowie Swimming Bath adjacent to the so-called Milton's Mulberry Tree, the scene of the crime as we shall see.

A. P. Baker, having heard the stories about the sightings of the apparition, began to use his fertile imagination to create the circumstances which could have caused this troubled spirit not to have rested in peace.

Baker then concocted the story in a series of connected, seemingly official, accounts and reports and newspaper stories all alluding to the death of a Christ's classics fellow from the 1850s named Philip Collier.

A colleague and rival of Collier's was another classics fellow named Christopher Round. They were not only rivals for academic honours but they were also rivals for the affections of a young and wealthy widow Lady Mary Clifford, who had moved into the manor house at Chesterton.

Frustratingly, Christopher Round, quite brilliant though he was, always came second to Collier in the various scholarship examinations they competed for, culminating in Collier securing the much sought-after University Chair of Greek Studies. And to add insult to injury, Collier shortly afterwards announced his engagement to Mary Clifford.

It must be pointed out at this juncture that Christopher Round considered himself the superior scholar but Philip Collier, although a quite brilliant scholar, had that magic ingredient: charisma, which swayed the examiners in closely contested situations.

It was at this point that Collier started behaving in what on the face of it seemed to be an intoxicated manner, returning to his rooms late at night via a gate in the Fellows' Garden from Parker's Piece, to avoid being observed by the porters. Christopher Round, from his rooms, would often observe Collier's clandestine entry into college, and his unsteady gait.

It was during one of these unsteady journeys across the Fellows' Gardens on a path by the swimming bath that the tragedy occurred. Collier lost his footing and fell into the swimming bath.

Christopher Round was doing his usual midnight perambulation round the garden when he observed Collier's mishap and believing him to need help, grabbed a pole with a hook on the end with the intention of extending it to the struggling Collier. However, he was suddenly seized with rage, "Why should I help this drunken buffoon who had caused me so much distress?" Instead, he smashed the hook onto Collier's head and saw him disappear beneath the water.

Christopher Round returned to his rooms and the experience of the night threw him into a fever and he became seriously ill. A nervous breakdown. The cure was a year away from Cambridge convalescing on the south coast.

On the fateful night, Collier's corpse was found on the path by the pool. Nobody suspected Christopher Round.

At the coroner's inquest, surprising evidence emerged in relation to Philip Collier's odd behaviour: he was taking part in experiments conducted by James Young Simpson, a doctor of medicine from Edinburgh University. He was endeavouring to invent an anaesthetic and, after returning to Edinburgh, developed chloroform. That was the explanation for Philip Collier's unsteady gait; he was still coming round from taking part in the experiments.

The reason Philip Collier became involved was to facilitate an operation that Mary Clifford desperately needed which could only be undertaken with her unconscious. Sadly, Simpson's discovery was too late to help Mary Clifford; she died not long after Philip Collier.

Christopher Round never really recovered from the events of that fateful night and spent the rest of his life as a humble tutor at Cambridge declining all appointments and preferments offered to him. The events of 29th May in the 1850s left an indelible and lasting impression on Christopher Round, and it is his ghost that is seen.

Amazingly all those witnessing the apparition testify to the sighting being on 29th May.

Separating fact from fiction is the subject of much learned discussion. There never were fellows at Christ's College named Christopher Round or Philip Collier. There really was a James Young Simpson who discovered chloroform at Edinburgh and was knighted. There is no record of him visiting Cambridge. The author of *A College Mystery*, A. P. Baker (1873–1919) really was a lecturer in history at Christ's College Cambridge. And who knows, perhaps Round and Collier were pseudonyms for two fellows of that period.

As for the ghost or apparition, the numerous sightings all bear the same description and in every case the date of the sightings: 29th May!

A CHINESE POET AT CAMBRIDGE (1922)

"Saying Goodbye to Cambridge Again" is, in many ways, the quintessential Cambridge poem, conveying its unique aura of the Backs and the River Cam and the golden willow trees. William Wordsworth's Cambridge poem was more about his alma mater St John's and Trinity College next door.

"Saying Goodbye to Cambridge Again" is described by almost everyone that reads it as beautiful. "Who wrote it?" they cry, "Keats, Shelley, Wordsworth?" The answer is, "No, Xu Zhimo" (1897–1931). "Who?" they declaim in disbelief.

Xu Zhimo, as a result of his short stay at King's College Cambridge (1921–1922), became China's leading romantic poet and a prominent member of "China's New Culture" in opposition to the Chinese Communist poets politically correct, prosaic form of poetry.

Until Cambridge, there was nothing. Xu was destined to follow his family's plans for him to enter their banking business.

To that end, he had attended various Chinese universities, and then to Clark University in New York to study banking, Columbia University to study economics and then to the London School of Economics in 1919 to 1920, from where he stole away briefly to Cambridge, to hear Bertrand Russell, the great philosopher's speech. He was determined to return.

He was already writing somewhat prosaic poetry and felt stifled at the LSE, as he had in America.

And it was to Cambridge that he fled, with the help of Cambridge historian Goldsworth Dickinson who arranged for him to spend a year at King's College as a "special student". It was here that he discovered his true self and became familiar with the works of Keats and Shelley.

As a special student who could sit in for any subject, he had the intellectual freedom without having to sit examinations. He went for long strolls, smoking and discussing literature and poetry over afternoon tea with his newly found English friends. Amongst these friends were intellectual icons G. L. Dickinson, E. M. Forster, Roger Fry, Edward Carter and Katherine Mansfield. He also attended lectures given by the philosopher Bertrand

Russell. Xu underwent a momentous transformation in his intellectual and literary pursuits. Cambridge really opened his eyes and transformed his thinking and Cambridge became *xiang* (native place), in reality his second home where he discovered the self that became the great Chinese romantic poet.

Like all great romantic poets, he had many affairs with women in America, England and his native China, in addition to two marriages. The emotional vicissitudes encountered in these liaisons were conducive to heartfelt romantic poetry.

His influence on modern Chinese poetry was profound, and his Cambridge poem and other writings created a literary Cambridge that more than any other place is Chinese readers' dreamland of the West.

He also translated the works of many English writers into Chinese, including William Blake, Thomas Hardy, Katherine Mansfield, Matthew Arnold and Christina Rossetti.

Cambridge really was Xu Zhimo's *xiang* and second home.

Sadly, he died in an aeroplane accident in 1931 at the young age of thirty-four. He had so much more still to give, but we must be grateful for all the poems and prose that he did write.

Saying Goodbye to Cambridge Again
Very quietly I take my leave
As quietly as I came here;
Quietly I wave goodbye
To the rosy clouds in the western sky.

The golden willows by the riverside
Are young brides in the setting sun;
Their reflections on the shimmering waves
Always linger in the depth of my heart.

The floating heart growing in the sludge
Sways leisurely under the water
In the gentle waves of Cambridge
I would be a water plant!

That pool under the shade of elm trees,
Holds not water but the rainbow from the sky;
Shattered to pieces among the duckweeds,
Is the sediment of a rainbow-like dream.

To seek a dream? Just to punt a boat upstream
To where the green grass is more verdant;
Or to have the boat fully loaded with starlight,
To sing aloud in the splendour of starlight.

But I cannot sing aloud,
Quietness is my farewell music;
Even summer insects keep silence for me;
Cambridge is soundless tonight!

Very quietly I take my leave
As quietly as I came here;
Gently I flick my sleeves.
Not even a wisp of cloud will I bring away.
(Xu Zhimo 1928)

FRANK WHITTLE - FATHER OF THE JET AGE (1927)

It was a sparkling autumnal day in October 1983; a glorious day for flying.

Captain Monty Cobby surveyed the list of passengers who would be flying on his Concorde flight that day, and one name amongst the up-market passengers caught his eye: Sir Frank Whittle. Captain Cobby glanced across the Concorde departure lounge and there was the great man, quietly reading The Times.

Unnoticed by the other passengers, this five feet three inches, thickset, elderly (seventy-six) gentleman, was suddenly descended upon by three BA executives and warmly greeted.

The other passengers now became curious, "Who was he? Must be important." In fact, they were in the presence of one of the most important men of the 20th century. He was the genius who invented the jet engine and they were about to travel on its most famous manifestation, Concorde, which would whisk them from Heathrow to Washington in three and a half hours.

Captain Cobby, by coincidence, had met Whittle a month earlier at a Concorde crew dinner at the Royal Air Force Club, where Whittle had given an unforgettable after dinner speech, about his life and work.

Frank Whittle was born on 1st June 1907, the son of a mechanic. At the age of fifteen, his initial attempts to join the RAF failed due to his lack of inches; he was only five feet tall. A crash programme of exercises rapidly elevated him to five feet three inches, which was deemed acceptable.

He entered the RAF as an apprentice in 1923, before being considered officer material in 1926 and transferred to Cranwell for training as a pilot. In fact, he was an exceptionally spectacular pilot and became part of the RAF's aerobatic display team. He was, in fact, too spectacular, destroying rather a lot of aircraft in attempting very risky manoeuvres. He was moved to the less risky job of pilot training.

It was during this time, aged only twenty, that he wrote his thesis entitled "Future Developments in Aircraft Design" in which he outlined his idea for using a gas turbine to produce jet propulsion. This, he argued, would propel a plane faster and higher, where the air resistance was of a lower magnitude, where it would operate more efficiently than the propeller-driven version, with its many more moving parts.

He tried to interest the Air Ministry but it thought

it impractical, but nevertheless he applied and obtained a patent for his revolutionary idea. Unfortunately, it was published in Germany. Within a year, a German engineer, Hans von Ohain, took up Whittle's design, generously backed by the Heinkel Aircraft Company.

In 1933, he was awarded an RAF scholarship to Peterhouse Cambridge where in only two years he gained a first in the Mechanical Science Tripos. Despite encouragement by the Head of Aeronautical Science, Melville Jones, the Air Ministry remained steadfastly opposed to the concept of the jet engine. This despite strong rumours emanating from Germany that it was embarking on its own jet programme.

Fortunately, three retired RAF officers, Williams, Tinling and Bramson, suggested that Whittle set up a development company with money borrowed from a small investment bank O. T. Falk. He borrowed £2,000 and in 1936 Power Jets was born. The Air Ministry grudgingly allowed him to be the company's part-time chief engineer. He was still a serving officer in the RAF.

Then one day in April 1937, in a ramshackle factory in Rugby, amongst clouds of smoke and deafening noise, parturition took place with the arrival of the jet engine. Hans von Ohain, however, beat Whittle to it, testing his first jet engine just one month earlier. With more than a little help from Heinkel, he had a jet plane, the HE 178, flying in August 1939. The news of this monumental event was enough to stir the Air Ministry from its sleepy reverie and it gave Power Jets the contract to build an engine around which the Gloster Aircraft Company would build an aeroplane. The Gloster E28/39 would be that aircraft. Due to further Air Ministry procrastination, the Gloster E28/39 did not fly until the 15th May 1941, nearly two years after the Heinkel.

By now it was evident to British engine manufacturers that the jet was the future, so tremendous pressure was put on the Air Ministry to let them all into the secret.

The Air Ministry now realised the potential of the jet engine and plans for a jet fighter were made, the Gloster Meteor, but Power Jets did not get the contract to build the engine, instead it went to the Rover Car Company. This proved to be a disaster. Two years were wasted whilst Rover inexplicably tried to redesign the engine. Rolls Royce came to the rescue and went back to Whittle's basic design. Five hundred Meteors were ordered and Meteor F1, using Whittle's own W28 engine, built by Rolls Royce as the Welland, entered service with No 616 Squadron RAF in July 1944. Later variants used the Rolls Royce Derwent engine. Altogether, including those in use with other nations, 3,941 Meteors were built over the course of the next twelve years.

The political infighting that followed the maiden jet flight of the Gloster E28/39 in May 1941 delayed the introduction into service of the Meteor by at least two years. Whittle did not want to surrender control, even though he wasn't an aircraft manufacturer. It was the appointment, in late 1942, of Stafford Cripps as Minister of Aircraft Production that provided the strategic skills necessary to produce a solution. Recognising that Power Jets' management was not equipped to run an aircraft manufacturer, he nationalised it and confined it to the role to which it and its charismatic leader Frank Whittle were uniquely suited: research and development.

Fortunately, von Ohain was having similar political problems in Germany and its first jet fighter didn't enter service until the same time as the Meteor, so neither country's jet planes played a significant part in World War II.

Instead, we handed over Whittle's plans to the Americans to kick-start its jet plane production. Whittle and a team of engineers went to America to help it develop its own engines. Whittle was greatly impressed with America's enthusiasm, a complete contrast to attitudes in Britain. We also sold fifteen Rolls Royce jet engines to the Russians who in turn passed them on to the Chinese. It powered the Soviet MIG 15, our adversary a few years later in the Korean War.

In 1948, Whittle was knighted and received £100,000 from the Royal Commission on Awards to Inventors. In that same year, Air Commodore Whittle was invalided out of the RAF. A disillusioned man constantly fighting battles with the establishment, he had suffered two nervous breakdowns.

After leaving the RAF, Sir Frank Whittle took up a professorship at the US Naval Academy.

He lived with his American wife in Maryland where he died in 1996, arguably one of the most important inventors of the 20th century.

He continued his connection with Cambridge when in 1972 the Whittle Research Laboratory was set up in west Cambridge sponsored by Rolls Royce. It is one of the world's leading aeronautical research establishments. Recently, Rolls Royce established a fellowship at his alma mater Peterhouse in his memory.

Perhaps his most significant accolade was from his German engineering adversary Hans von Ohain who observed that, "If the British establishment had the vision to back Whittle from the beginning, World War II would probably never had happened. Hitler would never have attempted his Luftwaffe invasion of Britain with a Royal Air Force equipped with jet-propelled planes."

CRADLE OF NOTABLE
20TH CENTURY WRITERS (1930)

Christ's College counts amongst its distinguished alumni the poet John Milton (1625–1632), the author of *Paradise Lost*.

Four hundred years later in the 20th century, Christ's produced several notable writers. C. P. Snow (later Lord Snow OBE) author of the quintessential Cambridge novel, *The Masters* (part of the Strangers and Brothers series of novels), who was a fellow of the college from 1930–1950. William Cooper (pen name of Harry Hoff) was a student at Christ's in the early 1930s and was a pupil of C. P. Snow. He was the author of *Scenes from Provincial Life*, thought by many to be the seminal influence on the new breed of "irreverent" post-war writers including John Osborne, John Braine, Alan Sillitoe, Malcolm Bradbury and Kingsley Amis, collectively labelled the "Angry Young Men" (derived from Osborne's play *Look Back in Anger*).

However, in terms of public recognition, it is another graduate from Christ's (1953), Colin Dexter OBE, who's probably the most famous, through his Inspector Morse novels which are set in the "other place" Oxford and have hardly been off the television screens for over thirty-five years.

CHRIST'S COLLEGE .HOME OF NOTABLE 20TH CENTURY WRITERS

THE BENSON DYNASTY (1940)

Edward White Benson (1829–1896) was the Archbishop of Canterbury from 1883 until his death from heart failure in 1896.

He was the eldest of eight children born to Edward White Benson Sr., a chemical engineer and manufacturer, and his wife Harriet (née Baker) in Highgate, Birmingham. He attended King Edward's School, Birmingham and then Trinity College Cambridge where he graduated with a BA in classics in 1852.

Whilst at Cambridge, he developed an interest in the paranormal, in particular investigating reports of ghosts. To this end, in 1851 he founded The Cambridge Association for Spiritual Inquiry, known informally as the "Cambridge Ghost Society". This bore fruit in literary form in 1895, when he was, by then, Archbishop of Canterbury, and recounted one of his ghostly investigations to the American writer Henry James. This became the inspiration of James' novella, *The Turn of the Screw*.

After leaving Cambridge in 1852, Benson began his career as a schoolmaster at the prestigious Rugby School, where he was ordained deacon in 1853 and priest in 1857. In 1859, he was appointed as the first Master of Wellington College in Berkshire, which was built by public subscription as a memorial to the Arthur Wellesley, first Duke of Wellington, who had died in 1852. He was a great soldier statesman, victor at Waterloo and twice prime minister of Great Britain.

In 1872, Benson embarked on his religious career as Chancellor of Lincoln Theological College. In 1877, he was appointed the first Bishop of Truro, where he served from 1877 to 1882. Amongst his most notable achievements when at Truro was the introduction of the "Festival of Nine Lessons and Carols", first used in Truro Cathedral on Christmas Eve 1880, which became the prototype for the world famous "Festival of Nine Lessons and Carols" at King's College, Cambridge which has been broadcast around the world every Christmas Eve since 1918.

In 1859, Edward Benson had married Mary Sidgwick, when she was only eighteen and he thirty. She was the daughter of Henry Sidgwick who, in 1859, cofounded Newnham College, the second Cambridge college after Girton to admit women.

The Bensons had six children and the surviving males all attended elite public schools before going on to

Cambridge. Their father died in 1896 and was buried in Canterbury Cathedral.

The sons all went on to make their mark in the literary world. The eldest, Arthur Christopher Benson (1862–1925), wrote the words to "Land of Hope and Glory" with music by Edward Elgar. It is the highlight of the Last Night at the Proms every year and is England's unofficial national anthem. After Eton, he was a scholar at King's College Cambridge. He went on to teach at Eton and then returned to Cambridge in 1904 as a fellow of Magdalene College, to lecture in English literature. He was master (head of college) of Magdalene from December 1915 until his death in 1925.

The fifth child of Edward White Benson was Edward Frederick Benson (1867–1940) who after Marlborough College progressed on to King's College Cambridge. He was a writer who achieved great acclaim with his Mapp and Lucia novels, which were turned into a popular television series in the 1980s. The setting for the majority of the novels was the fictional Tilling, in reality Rye in Sussex, where he lived in Lamb House which was formerly owned by the great family friend, American novelist Henry James. He loved Rye and was mayor of the town for three years in the 1920s. He wrote many novels, including *Dodo*, another comedy of manners like Mapp and Lucia.

The youngest of the Benson's children was Robert Hugh Benson (1871–1914) who after attending Eton and Trinity College Cambridge became an English Anglican priest. In 1903, he was received into the Roman Catholic church and ordained as a priest in 1904. He was a prolific writer like his brothers, writing much ghost and horror fiction. His most notable novel was *Lord of the World*.

None of the brothers married as they were all homosexuals, but they all made their mark in the literary world and all were, like their father, Cantabrians.

ROSALIND FRANKLIN –
THE UNSUNG HEROINE OF DNA (1953)

In early 1953, Maurice Wilkins of King's College London wrote to Francis Crick at the Cavendish Laboratories in Cambridge to announce "our dark lady is leaving us next week". The lady in question was Wilkins' colleague at King's, Rosalind Franklin.

They had been working together along with Francis Crick and James Watson from Cambridge on the structure of DNA. Wilkins then went on to say that as soon as she was gone they could "go full steam ahead with solving the structure of the DNA molecule that lies in every gene, free from her obstructiveness".

Wilkins then showed to Crick and Watson some of Franklin's unpublished data, including the crucial photo 51. This X-ray diffraction picture of a DNA model was Watson's inspiration. Using Rosalind Franklin's photograph and their own data, Watson, Crick and Wilkins created their famous DNA model.

This was famously announced to the world by Francis Crick in The Eagle hostelry in Cambridge, one lunchtime in February 1953. As a result, in public perception it became Crick and Watson's discovery, although eight years' later the Nobel Prize was awarded to Crick, Watson and Wilkins.

Rosalind Franklin's contribution to the DNA model was not acknowledged at the time, but in 1958 when she tragically died from ovarian cancer, Francis Crick acknowledged her crucial contribution.

Who was this unsung heroine who aroused such obloquy from her colleague Maurice Wilkins?

Rosalind Franklin was born on 25th July 1920 in Notting Hill, London into an affluent and influential British Jewish family. Her father was a politically liberal London merchant banker who taught at the city's Working Men's College. She was the second of five children.

Rosalind attended St Paul's Girls' School where she excelled in science and sports. She topped her class and went on to Newnham College Cambridge in 1938, where she studied chemistry and was awarded a second class honours degree from her final exams. She was awarded a research fellowship at Newnham and completed her thesis as research officer with the British Coal Utilisation Research Association; she was awarded her PhD by Cambridge in 1945.

In late 1946, she secured an appointment with the State Chemical Laboratory in Paris, where she worked with crystallographer Jacques Mering. He taught her X-ray diffraction, which would prove crucial in her later work on the structure of DNA. She loved France and the way of life in Paris, and was able to indulge her passion for the great outdoors hiking over the Alps.

Despite her attachment to France, she returned to England in January 1951 to take up an appointment as a research associate at King's College London and used her expertise and X-ray diffraction techniques to study DNA structure. She made an amazing discovery: DNA had two forms, a dry A form and a wet B form. One of the B form diffraction pictures, known as photograph 51, became famous as critical evidence in identifying the structure of DNA.

However, her stay at King's College was a short one owing to a clash of personalities with Maurice Wilkins, a shy, meek man who hated debate and vigorous argument. Rosalind was the opposite; she loved any sort of debate whether scientific or political, and could not suffer fools gladly. She was also diligent and a perfectionist. And this is where sexism reared its ugly head because Watson also found her "difficult to work with". She did not get the credit at the time for her critical contribution to the "secret of life" DNA discovery.

In any case, she had moved on to Birkbeck College where she excelled, making many trips to America where she renewed her acquaintance with Donald Casper, who had worked with Rosalind at Birkbeck College and was to become a fellow of the Academy of Art and Sciences. She admitted just before her death that Casper was the one whom she might have loved and might have married.

One rather sad but poignant footnote is that her ovarian cancer may have been related to the hundreds of hours she spent exposed to the harmful effects of X-rays.

The lack of recognition at the time for probably the most important female scientist to graduate from Cambridge has been rectified in the 21st century by a number of biographies, most notably *Rosalind Franklin: The Dark Lady of DNA* written by Brenda Maddox.

MORSE CREATOR COLIN DEXTER – CAMBRIDGE'S GIFT TO OXFORD (1953)

The television series *Inspector Morse* starring John Thaw is, according to a poll conducted by the Radio Times, the most popular television detective series ever. It has been shown in no less than 200 countries around the world, and spawned a sequel, *Lewis*, and a prequel, *Endeavour*. Altogether, the Morse industry has run more or less continuously for thirty-five years.

It has not only turned Oxford into the murder capital of Europe but also helped make it into one of Britain's top tourist attractions.

The original television series was adapted from the crime novels of Colin Dexter, who was made an OBE in 2000 for his services to literature and awarded the freedom of the city of Oxford in 2001. He wrote thirteen Morse novels, all of which were included in the thirty-three episodes of the Morse television series, first broadcast between 1987 and 2000. Both the books and the television plays were characterised by their clever plots and numerous red herrings, and, of course, the physical presence of Oxford with its magnificent and varied architecture, famously referred to as the "city of dreaming spires" by Matthew Arnold in his poem "Thyrsis".

It therefore comes as a great shock when it is revealed that Colin Dexter was a graduate of Christ's College Cambridge. Given the great rivalry that exists between Britain's two oldest universities, how could such an enormous act of disloyalty have occurred? Why couldn't Morse have joined the Cambridgeshire Constabulary; after all, Dexter was thoroughly familiar with Cambridge and its environs, its architecture and scenery, which are equal if not superior to Oxford in splendour, particularly the Backs and the River Cam.

Colin Dexter was one of three children born to Alfred and Dorothy Dexter. His father and mother left school at the age of twelve and Alfred was a taxi driver. Colin obtained a scholarship to Stamford School, a minor public school, where he excelled in the classics, Greek and Latin.

On leaving school with his A levels, he did national service where he prophetically became a Morse code specialist. He then entered Christ's College Cambridge where he read classics, graduating in 1953 with a BA, which duly became an MA in 1958.

Colin then taught classics at various schools in eastern England before becoming senior classics teacher at Corby Grammar School in Northamptonshire. He was forced to give up teaching in 1966 due to his incipient deafness. And this is where fate intervened, because he managed to secure a post with the Oxford Examining Board, which entailed him moving to Oxford with his wife Dorothy and his two young children.

It was during this period that he began writing in his spare time, publishing his first Morse crime novel *Last Bus to Woodstock* in 1975.

In 1988, at the age of fifty-eight, he was forced into early retirement by his deteriorating hearing, despite four unsuccessful operations. By this time, he had written seven of the thirteen Morse novels as a part-time writer.

His early retirement not only allowed him to become a full-time author, but retirement also gave him the time to pursue a semi-theatrical career addressing charity events, as well as appearing at theatres doing "Morse and Me" evenings and giving literary readings with seasoned professionals.

He shared many of Morse's tastes such as his love of Wagner, poetry, crosswords, real ale and whisky. Colin Dexter was national crossword champion on a number of occasions, alternating with his great friend and rival Sir Jeremy Morse, the chairman of Lloyds Bank after whom he eponymously named his great fictional creation.

One final plea in the defence of his decision to choose Oxford over Cambridge as the setting for the Morse novels was the ease with which he could do the legwork for the sometimes obscure settings for his stories, such as Holywell Cemetery, Wytham Wood, Jericho, numerous pubs and, of course, the Oxford colleges and university buildings such as the Sheldonian and St Mary's Church. These are a cinematographer's dream, being so photogenic, so much so that Oxford became a central character. Add to that the musical score and haunting theme tune by Barrington Pheloung and you have, along with the memorable Morse and Lewis characterisations, all the ingredients for the most successful crime series ever to be shown on national television.

Colin lived in the same semi-detached house in north Oxford on the Banbury Road from 1966 until his death in March 2017. He also drove the same old Metro for many years, but as he would explain he didn't really need a car preferring to use public transport, particularly if he was drinking.

Apart from the public honours, he also received professional honours from the Crime Writers' Association for his books: two silver daggers, two gold daggers and a Cartier diamond dagger for lifetime achievement.

He truly was an Oxbridge man; Cambridge's gift to Oxford and the world.

MORSE CREATOR COLIN DEXTER WITH THE ACTOR JOHN THAW ,
WHO IMMORTALISED HIM ON TV.

THE CAMBRIDGE DON WHO BECAME A TELEVISION STAR (1955)

Glyn Daniel was a Welsh archaeologist and fellow of St John's College Cambridge, who is credited with bringing archaeology to the world.

Through his frequent appearances on television with Sir Mortimer Wheeler, most notably *Animal, Vegetable, Mineral?* and *Buried Treasure* between 1952 and 1959, he became one of the most recognisable people on television. He even received the accolade of Television Personality of the Year in 1955.

It must be remembered that at this time there was only one channel to watch on television, the BBC, until 1955 when ITV was launched, so Glyn Daniel had an ideal monopolistic platform to introduce archaeology to the masses. After the launch of ITV, he was, in 1959, appointed a director of Anglia Television, a post he held for twenty years. In that time, he made sure that archaeology featured prominently in its schedules.

This apparently glamorous world of living in the public limelight was a far cry from his childhood in the villages of Lampeter Velfrey in Pembrokeshire and later Llantwit Major in the Vale of Glamorgan, where life was dominated by chapel and church music. His father was a schoolmaster, as well as deacon and choirmaster at the village chapel, and Glyn Daniel learnt to play the harmonium. Importantly to his future development, Llantwit Major was on the Jurassic Coast and was one of the major areas for fossils dating back 200 million years. As a child, he took a great interest in these archaeological treasures, and thus began a lifelong fascination with archaeology, allied to a lifelong love of church music, and in particular organ and choral music.

From the age of eleven, Glyn Daniel attended Barry County School, where his academic brilliance led him to be awarded a state scholarship and a Glamorgan County scholarship. On the strength of the latter, he attended Cardiff University where he studied geography, and church organ at Llandaff Cathedral under Dr George Beale. Beale taught him the whole repertoire of organ music, but had to tell him that he was not gifted enough to make it a career.

After one year at Cardiff, courtesy of his state scholarship, he transferred to St John's College Cambridge to study archaeology, then a minority subject which he was about to change, thanks to a childhood surrounded by its manifestations. In 1935, he graduated with a first class honours degree with distinction in archaeology. He then took his doctorate where he chose for his thesis megalithic monuments in southern Britain. He borrowed his father's car for three years in order to tour all the known sites in southern Wales and England. Just as well he was an only child!

Glyn Daniel was to spend the rest of his working life, over forty years, at St John's, save for the interruption of the Second World War, where he became a fellow and tutor until his retirement in 1981.

During the Second World War, he applied his talents interpreting archaeological sites from aerial photography, working for the RAF reconnaissance unit at RAF Medmenham in Buckinghshire, the RAF's main interpretation centre for photo reconnaissance interpretation operations in Europe. He was a key figure in its work and recruited and taught other archaeologists to adapt their talents to war work. This proved to be useful experience for his later work teaching and lecturing at university.

Such was his success at Medmenham, he was, in 1942, sent to India to set up the Central Photographic Centre in Delhi, covering the Far East and Asia. This was as a result of Japan entering the war. He was to remain in India for the duration of the war, a period he was later to describe as one of comparative comfort and relaxation.

So much so that he wrote his first two books during this time, *The Cambridge Murders*, a detective story, and *100 Years of Archaeology*. In addition to many archaeological books, he went on to write a second detective novel, *Welcome Death*.

Daniel achieved the rank of Wing Commander and fell in love with one of his staff WAAF officers, Ruth Langhorne, a product of St Anne's College Oxford whom he married in 1946. With a degree in geography, she was to prove invaluable to his publishing endeavours for the next forty years.

THE MOST INGENIOUS
STUDENT PRANK EVER (1958)

On 8th June 1958, one of the most ingenious student pranks ever, the placing of an Austin Seven on the roof of the university's Senate House building, was perpetrated in the centre of Cambridge. It required a high degree of mechanical engineering skill.

Such a feat should come as no surprise, as Cambridge has always led the world in the field of physical sciences, of which engineering is a key part. Isaac Newton (laws of gravity), Frank Whittle (inventor of the jet engine), Christopher Cockerell (inventor of the Hovercraft), Alan Turing (general purpose computer) are just a few of the representatives of this proud tradition. All Cambridge alumni.

The student prank was perpetrated by undergraduates of Gonville and Caius College, led by Peter Davey. At the time, it was not known who had been responsible for the outrageous prank. But in 2008, fifty years later, the shadowy group of engineering students reunited and disclosed their identities and revealed how they winched an Austin Seven to the top of the university's seventy feet high Senate House.

At an anniversary dinner in June 2008, ringleader Peter Davey revealed that he had hatched the plan while staying in rooms at Gonville and Caius College, overlooking the Senate House roof. He felt the expanse of roof "cried out" to be made more interesting and decided a car would do the trick, so he recruited eleven other engineering students to help realise his plan.

The group chose May Bumps week when any passersby along King's Parade were likely to be drunken rowers, celebrating after their exertions.

They found a clapped-out Austin Seven and towed it through Cambridge to a parking space near the Senate House. On the fateful night, they manoeuvered the car into position, and a lifting party on the Senate House roof hoisted it up using an A-shaped crane constructed from scaffolding poles "borrowed" from King's College next door, and steel ropes supplied by the local rowing club.

Another group, the bridge party, passed a plank across the eight-foot wide Senate Passage, which runs between Gonville and Caius College and the Senate House. This was used by the lifters to ferry across lifting gear comprising ropes, hooks and pulleys. The engine of the Austin Seven was removed to make it lighter. It was lifted and swung through the A-frame and pushed to the apex of the roof by the bridge party before they beat a hasty retreat over the plank bridge.

The next morning, the sight of the Austin Seven on the Senate roof enthralled crowds of onlookers, as attempts by the authorities to construct a crane to hoist the car back down failed. They ended up using blowtorches to cut the car into pieces in order to remove it. The intrepid twelve could have got the car back down in one piece, but were fearful of being expelled, so they kept mum.

HOW ON EARTH DID THEY DO THAT!

The then dean of Caius, the late Reverend Hugh Montefiore, had an inkling of who was responsible, and sent a case of champagne to the pranksters' staircase, while maintaining in public that he knew nothing of the culprits. He was clearly proud of his college's great engineering feat, because it reinforced the university's great engineering tradition.

The ringleader Peter Davey from Mousehole, Cornwall was awarded a CBE and an honorary doctorate after setting up automation and robotic companies during his working life. He died in September 2016 and will be forever remembered as the instigator of the most ingenious student prank ever.

THE FOOTLIGHTS AND THE SATIRE BOOM (1960)

Ground-breaking is an appropriate description for the productions of the Cambridge University Students' "Footlights" in the late 1950s and early 1960s, which were the catalysts for the anti-establishment "satire boom". Its production of *The Last Laugh* in 1959, written by Peter Cook and John Fortune, and performed by Cook, Timothy Birdsall and Eleanor Bron, really put the "Footlights" on the map nationally. After appearing at the Theatre Royal Cambridge, it then went on to the Edinburgh Festival Fringe, before transferring to the West End in London.

Such was its success, that a revue entitled *Beyond the Fringe* was conceived, combining the best of the Cambridge and Oxford talents: Peter Cook and Jonathan Miller (students from Cambridge Footlights), Dudley Moore and Alan Bennett (students at Oxford University) and members of the Oxford Revue. *Fringe* was written by all four, who also performed in its debut at the Edinburgh Festival Fringe in August 1960, before it transferred to London's Fortune Theatre, where it received rave reviews. From there, it travelled to New York where it appeared on Broadway and the Ed Sullivan Show, and received a full-page review in Time Magazine. It was a huge success in New York and was the "must-see" show, with President Kennedy amongst its audience.

The satire boom was well and truly launched, and the Footlights became a national institution.

Founded in 1883 as an amateur theatre club by Cambridge University students, it quickly changed its focus to comedy and each year produced a revue which appeared at Cambridge's Theatre Royal, and then after its foundation in 1947 at the annual Edinburgh Festival Fringe. In essence, it was no more than an "end of pier concert party", and it trundled along in this mode for the next eighty years.

Then in the late 1950s and early 1960s, a unique intake of students to Cambridge University transformed the Footlights with their sheer talent and brilliance. Amongst them were Peter Cook, Jonathan Miller, John Bird, John Fortune, David Frost, Eleanor Bron, Timothy Birdsall and John Cleese. They were satire's early pioneers and went on to establish themselves in the performing arts and writing in such shows as *The Goodies*, *Monty Python's Flying Circus* and *Not So Much a Programme More a Way of Life* and, of course, *Fawlty Towers*. But that's another story.

The success of *Beyond the Fringe* was based on its

lampooning of politicians and establishment figures as never before. Peter Cook, the driving force behind the satire boom, in 1961 opened the Establishment Club in Greek Street London, showcasing jazz and satire.

This was quickly followed by the launch of the magazine "Private Eye", famous for its satire and investigative journalism. Again Peter Cook was involved, providing much-needed funding in the early days. It was famous for revealing the misdoings of powerful business tycoons such as Robert Maxwell and James Goldsmith and consequently received regular libel writs. Today it is Britain's top-selling current affairs magazine and is hugely profitable.

Then in 1962 was launched probably the most controversial and outrageous television programme ever, *That Was the Week That Was*. It was hosted by an unknown former Cambridge Footlights member, twenty-three-year old David Frost. Again, like "Private Eye", it was famous for lampooning politicians and other leading figures, particularly Prime Minister Harold Macmillan. Other performers included Roy Kinnear, Lance Percival, Willy Rushton and Millicent Martin. They all went on to successful careers in the performing arts. Its writers included Keith Waterhouse, Johnny Speight, Graham Chapman and the ubiquitous Peter Cook. As might be imagined, it received a vast number of complaints, particularly from Conservative politicians. It was taken off the air at the end of 1963 because of the looming general election.

Its presenter David Frost went on to become a household name with programmes like *The Frost Report*. But it was as an interviewer of leading world politicians such as disgraced US ex-President Nixon that he is chiefly remembered. Altogether, he interviewed all serving American presidents in office between 1969 and 2008, as well as all eight British prime ministers in office between 1964 and 2016. He was knighted in 1996 and died of a heart attack in 2013 at the age of seventy-four, whilst on a lecture cruise.

The Footlights' luminaries and instigators of the satire boom with *Beyond the Fringe*, went on to achieve fame in their separate television and theatrical careers. Peter Cook wrote two West End reviews for Kenneth Williams: *Pieces of Eight* and *One Over the Eight*, and teamed up with Dudley Moore to make two television series: *Not Only But Also* and *Pete and Dud*. They split up in 1970 due to Peter Cook's increasing problems with alcohol, which eventually led to his early death at the age of fifty-seven. Jonathan Miller, after training in medicine and specialising in neurology, went on to have an immensely successful career as an English theatre and opera director, actor, author, television presenter and humorist. He died in 2019 at the age of eighty-five. He was knighted in 2002.

Today, the inheritors of the "Fringe" satire legacy are the immensely popular and long-running television programmes *Spitting Image* and *Have I Got News for You.*

KING'S COLLEGE'S CROWNING GLORY (1961)

It is an established fact that the universities of Oxford and Cambridge and their individual colleges possess a combined wealth of £20.6 billion, which is more than all the other twenty-two members of the elite Russell Group of universities combined.

The wealthiest college is Trinity, Cambridge, whose assets are worth an estimated £1.4 billion, and these values do not include the freehold value of their sites.

It is a moot question as to what value they have put on their considerable collection of works of art, particularly paintings.

One case in point is the magnificent Paul Rubens' "Adoration of the Magi", which is an altarpiece in King's College Chapel, Cambridge. It measures 4.2 metres by 3.2 metres (13 feet 9 inches by 10 feet 6 inches) and was acquired as a gift from a property developer, Major Alfred Allnatt, in 1961. He had acquired the painting at an auction in 1959 for £275,000 (then a world record for a painting). It was in 1974 valued at £1 million (equivalent to £6 million today).

THE PRICELESS RUBÉN'S

Such was its value both intrinsically and as a "priceless" work of art that, after being initially housed in the antechapel, it was decided that the east end of the main chapel would be modified so it could be installed as an altarpiece. The floor at the east end was lowered by removing three steps up to the altar, so the painting did not obscure the chapel's stained glass windows. Also removed were wooden railings, oak panelling, a communion rail and reredos, and Tudor panelling. Needless to say the changes were, and still are, controversial. The perceived wisdom was that the removal of the irreplaceable features was to improve the visual impact on TV when the annual "Festival of Nine Lessons and Carols" was broadcast on Christmas Eve! But it also demonstrates the immense value put on the Rubens by the college authorities, as one of the jewels in the college's crown.

DNA PIONEER PROPOSES A BROTHEL AND NOT A CHAPEL FOR NEW COLLEGE (1961)

In a speech to the Massachusetts Institute of Technology in March 1949, Sir Winston Churchill observed that, "we have suffered in Great Britain by the lack of universities and colleges in which engineering, science and technology are taught".

When he ceased to be prime minister, he decided to correct this omission by launching, in 1958, a scheme to establish Churchill College Cambridge.

The first undergraduates were admitted in 1961 and, importantly, the college statutes required that 70% of the undergraduates should be studying science or technology.

However, against the background of the new college's "brave new world", there was unleashed the mother and father of all intellectual battles so beloved by academics. Should the college have a chapel?

The atheist dons at the college led by DNA pioneer Francis Crick said that, in the mid 20th century, an institution dedicated to science and technology had no business supporting superstitious nonsense. Those dons who were Christians insisted that the college should have a chapel.

To support his opposition, Francis Crick, in 1961, wrote a letter to Sir Winston Churchill, who was chairman of the College's Trustees, suggesting that he set up a brothel, as it would serve the college better than a chapel. He also enclosed a cheque for ten guineas towards its cost.

The cheque was returned without comment.

In the end, a compromise was reached with the help of Lord Anthony Beaumont an Anglican priest and liberal politician, who agreed to finance the entire cost of the chapel.

A trust was set up which leased from the college a small piece of land on the periphery of the forty-acre college site on which a chapel would be built. In the words of a former vice-master of Churchill, Mark Goldie, there is a chapel *at* Churchill, but there is no chapel *of* Churchill.

Even Crick compromised and accepted an honorary fellowship in 1965, although he turned down a knighthood for his DNA work, because he disapproved of kings and queens!

CHURCHILL COLLEGE CHAPEL NOT A BROTHEL

A COLLEGE LIKE NO OTHER –
A VISUAL DELIGHT (1965)

Walking up the steep ascent of Castle Street from Magdalene Bridge, passing Castle Mound and Shire Hall on the right, you cross at the traffic lights and the road becomes Madingley Road, and immediately on the left you are confronted with what appears to be a sultan's palace or a Byzantine church; a white, twin-domed building which is the centrepiece of Murray Edwards College, which architecturally is like no other university building in Britain, let alone Cambridge. It is stunning!

It has cheekily been suggested that the proposed new college had a very limited budget, and to save money was persuaded by the architects to use an existing design which had been rejected by a Middle Eastern sultan, who had changed his mind and wanted his new palace to be of a Gothic character. The veracity of this ingenious tale cannot be confirmed. But it would certainly have met the budget constraints of the new college.

In 1952, the association to promote a third foundation for women in Cambridge was set up. By 1954, £25,000 had been secured and a postal ballot of association members had produced a name: New Hall.

The college was known as New Hall until 2008 when, as a result of a donation of £30 million by a former student, Ross Edwards, it was changed to Murray Edwards. The Murray part of the name was to honour Dame Rosemary Murray (1913–2004) who was the college's first president (1954–1981) and was also the first woman to hold the post of vice-chancellor of the University of Cambridge.

The new college was opened in October 1954, with sixteen graduates in the Hermitage on Silver Street, which is now part of Darwin College.

By 1962, a total of £220,000 had been received from the Wolfson Foundation and the Elizabeth Nuffield Foundation. Additionally, the Darwin family (descendants of Charles Darwin of *On the Origin of Species* fame) generously gave the college a gift of land on the Madingley Road, half a mile north of the city centre.

The college authorities appointed as architects the firm of Chamberlain, Powell and Bon and as their first president, Miss Rosemary Murray. The new site was opened in June 1965 by Queen Elizabeth, the Queen Mother.

The visual impact of Murray Edwards is defined by the magnificent domed dining hall, which seems to rise from the waters of Fountain Court. The concrete petalled dome was, with its Byzantine connotations, designed by Peter Chamberlain to echo Corbusier's landmark chapel at Ronchamp in France.

Completed in 1965 and now a Grade II listed building, it was the precursor to Chamberlain's more famous work: that concrete masterpiece that is the Barbican Centre in London.

MURRAY EDWARDS . AN ARCHITECTURAL DELIGHT.

One unique feature in the dining hall is the serving bar which rises up through the opening floor like a scene from *Star Trek*. It is still in good working order, but it is only activated on special occasions.

Murray Edwards is definitely one of the architectural gems of Cambridge, with its Byzantine dome and buildings of white brick and prestressed concrete.

THE CRAZY DIAMOND AND PINK FLOYD (1965)

"Remember when you were young You shone like the sun Shine on, you crazy diamond Now there's a look in your eyes Like black holes in the sky Shine on, you crazy diamond."

"Shine On You Crazy Diamond" is a nine-part song by the legendary Cambridge rock band, Pink Floyd. It was featured on their 1975 album "Wish You Were Here", as a tribute to the band's enigmatic founder Syd Barrett, the creator of the band's unique psychedelic style.

Syd Barrett, having founded the band with Roger Waters in 1965 and recruited Nick Mason (drums) and Richard Wright (keyboards) to the line-up, was the driving force initially. He wrote and was lead vocalist on their earliest hits: "See Emily Play", "Arnold Layne" and "Bike" all featured on Pink Floyd's first album released in 1967, "Piper at the Gates of Dawn".

Very much inspired by The Beatles, they were one of the first British psychedelic groups, distinguished by extended compositions and concept albums.

Syd Barrett was heavily into recreational drugs, such as LSD, and became increasingly dependent and dysfunctional on them, so much so that David Gilmour was recruited in 1968 to cover for him, when he failed to turn up for performances.

Barrett, Waters and Gilmour met when attending nearby schools in Hill Road, Cambridge: the Perse School and Cambridge High. They were all from middle-class professional families.

In April 1968, five months after Gilmour joined the group, Barrett was ousted from the band because of his unreliability, due to what amounted to a nervous breakdown.

After Syd Barrett left the group, Roger Waters became the creative force and lead vocalist and they released a string of concept albums which were received to great critical acclaim: "Dark Side of the Moon" (1973), "Wish You Were Here" (1975), "Animals" (1977) and "The Wall" (1979).

By the time "The Wall" was released, Pink Floyd were one of the biggest rock bands on the planet, surpassed only by The Beatles and Led Zeppelin. They have sold more than 250 million records worldwide and their live shows were a mind-blowing experience, with special lighting and sound effects including helicopters and aeroplanes flying across the arena on wires.

Roger Waters left the band in 1985 because of

irreconcilable differences with David Gilmour, saying as his parting shot that "Pink Floyd were a spent force creatively" (without him) and should be wound up. However, Gilmour and the other two members didn't agree and went on to make three more highly successful albums: "Momentary Lapse of Reason" (1987), "The Division Bell" (1994) and "The Endless River" (2014).

PINK FLOYDS FIRST ALBUM WITH SYD BARRETT

The highlights of the Gilmour period were the ever more complex live shows in large arenas such as Earls Court. They ceased performing as a group in 1995, but briefly reformed in 2005 for a global live aid performance. Sadly, the antipathy between Waters and Gilmour is still a running sore, making it unlikely that they will ever perform together again, although Waters has pursued a solo career and still continues to perform live even though he is in his late 70s.

Altogether, Pink Floyd released fifteen studio albums and nine compilation and live performance albums over a period of fifty-two years.

Syd Barrett (the crazy diamond) pursued a solo career for a short while after leaving Pink Floyd, and after two solo albums, disappeared from the music scene. His last public performance was at the Cambridge Corn Exchange in 1972. He became a virtual recluse occupying his time with painting and gardening. He died of pancreatic cancer in 2006 at the age of sixty.

THE WINDOW CLEANER'S
FIVE MINUTES OF FAME (1970)

The main entrance to Trinity College Cambridge is the Great Gate in Trinity Street where in a niche above the entrance is a statue of Henry VIII, who founded the college in 1546.

The statue is the cause of much amusement amongst the hordes of visitors who "crocodile tail" around Cambridge each year in the company of one of the many Cambridge guides. The reason for this merriment is the chair leg which Henry holds in his right hand, where once had been a sceptre. In his left hand, he quite properly holds an orb.

How did a chair leg come to be there in the first place, spoiling the dignity of such a formidable monarch? A student prank is the most obvious claim. But when? And in any case, other objects have appeared in Henry's hand during the latter part of the 20th century: a bicycle pump, a skull and other versions of the chair leg. It is totally baffling.

Then, in 1998, a letter appeared in CAM, the university magazine, which explained, in effect, how easy it would be to have removed the sceptre.

The letter was from Dr Clifford Evans, a distinguished fellow at St John's College, Trinity's next-door neighbour, who revealed that in the early 1950s, craftsmen from St John's maintenance department were asked by Trinity to make a replacement sceptre for the one held by Henry which had rotted away to a mere stump. Being made of heart oak, this was bound to happen over time. The stump was easily removed because it fitted into a cylindrical sleeve in the statue's hand. Dr Evans, who was at the time junior bursar at St John's, inspected the stump and maintains that it was not part of a chair leg. A replica of the sceptre was duly made and gilded and fixed into the cylindrical sleeve.

Thus it explains why the sceptre was subsequently so frequently removed and replaced by other objects such as a bicycle pump, skull and chair leg.

An old sepia photograph from the 1850s quite clearly shows a sceptre crowned with a fleur-de-lis. A later photograph from 1923 shows a sceptre reduced to only the shortest stem, which supports Dr Clifford's assertion that there had never been a chair leg in Henry's hand until after the 1950s replica was placed in the monarch's hand.

Nevertheless, even if after the 1950s, the appearance of the chair leg was still a student prank.

THE TRINITY GATEHOUSE STATUE OF HENRY VIII
WITH A CHAIRLEG IN RIGHT HAND.

However, even this exciting notion was dispelled when a retired employee of the Chesterton Window Cleaning Company, Peter Binge, in 2010 admitted to the Cambridge Evening News and the Varsity Magazine that he was the culprit.

Apparently, he had been cleaning the windows in the Gate House Tower when he noticed that Henry VIII's statue did not have the sceptre in his hand. He assumed it had been removed as a student prank. So, Mr Binge did no more than pop into the staircase of the Gate House Tower where he remembered seeing a discarded broken chair outside one of the rooms. He took a leg off and popped it into the monarch's right hand. It fitted perfectly. And as far as anybody knows, it has remained there until the present day.

The Trinity authorities had seriously thought of replacing the chair leg with another replica of the sceptre but, like its predecessor, it would likely be removed. And in any case, it's such a great tourist attraction.

THE CAMBRIDGE RAPIST (1975)

In mid June 1975, Flora Hinton visited her parents for the weekend in their home in Cambridge. Their conversation was dominated by the story which had received nationwide coverage, concerning the activities of the so-called Cambridge Rapist. The city was in a state of apprehension and fear about an unknown man who, between October 1974 and June 1975, raped no less than six women.

On a more pleasant note, Flora's parents waxed lyrical about their handyman Peter Cook, who had installed some elaborate bookcases in the study and repaired a valuable military chest in one of the bedrooms. Not only that, he had also heroically dived into the nearby River Cam to rescue her six-year-old nephew, who had fallen into the Cam from a punt. However, the police kept rearresting him because, in his own words, "I'm a little fella like the rapist and I got into trouble with the police when I was a youth; they've got it in for me". Flora's mother was very sympathetic to this apparent unfair treatment of their heroic handyman.

The Cambridge Rapist's reign of terror had begun on 18th October 1974. A young student was alone in the house she shared with four other students in Springfield Road, half a mile from Jesus College where she was an undergraduate. She had just emerged from the bath clad only in a towel when the lights suddenly went out and a short, stocky man burst through the door and roughly pushed her to the ground. He then tied her wrists together with her own blouse, and said to her, "I came to rob you, but I think I will rape you". She was savagely raped and robbed of £12 from her purse.

Thus begun the succession of rapes, amounting to six in all between October 1974 and June 1975. They all followed the same pattern, growing ever more savage with some victims being stabbed in the stomach before being raped.

Despite the biggest police manhunt ever mounted in Britain, they were, by June 1975, no nearer to catching the rapist. They now had forensic evidence from the rapist left at the scenes of the crimes: his blood group which was O, and his semen which revealed that the rapist was sterile (firing blanks). The police invited all males aged between thirty and fifty, and around five feet tall to come forward, so they could be eliminated and 1,644 did, but not the rapist.

Meanwhile, Mrs Hinton's ear was being bent by Peter Cook bewailing the fact that he and his adoring wife could not have children.

The rapist was getting evermore bold and had taken to wearing a mask with the word "RAPIST" written across the forehead. When escaping from the scenes of his rapes, he donned a blond wig and wore women's clothes, because he knew the police were looking for a man. He also used a woman's bicycle when carrying out his rapes, because Cambridge was a city of student bicycles, and a blond-haired woman on a bicycle would not be unusual.

Meanwhile, on the Saturday afternoon of her weekend visit, Flora Hinton, alone in her parent's home, received a visit from her parents' handyman Peter Cook, whose first question was, "Are your parents in?" On hearing that she was on her own, and after hesitating for a moment, he pushed passed her quite roughly, saying he wanted to check the shelves he had put up a few days earlier. Halfway down the hallway, he turned round having changed his mind. "No, I meant I wanted to check that they were satisfied with the military chest I repaired". "Let me show you, it's in the top bedroom." Flora now began to feel really uneasy. Just then the phone rang and when she returned, Cook was gone.

A week later, the rapist's reign of terror came to an end in the early hours of Sunday 8th June 1975. A twenty-eight-year-old Canadian exchange student was asleep in Owlstone Croft Hostel near Selwyn College, when she was awakened in the early hours by footsteps in the corridor outside her room. When she opened the door to see who was there, the rapist lunged at her, but her screams caused him to flee. Two anglers night-fishing on the nearby River Cam heard the woman's screams and ran towards the hostel, one of them alerting a passing policeman. An urgent message went out to all undercover units in the area.

In nearby Selwyn Road, Detective Constable Terry Edwards had just received an all alerts radio message at 2:35 a.m., when he heard the sound of a bicycle coming towards him, ridden by a woman with long blond hair. It had no lights, despite it being a pitch-black night. DC Edwards requested the cyclist to stop. She swerved round him, but Edwards managed to grab her hair, which came off in his hand, and caused the cyclist to crash to the ground, unbalanced by his lunge.

Restrained by Edwards and nearby residents who had come out of their homes to see what all the commotion was about, they soon discovered that she was a he, and he was arrested and taken to the nearest police station. The police searched his bags and found they contained more women's clothes, as well as a torch, a knife, a jemmy (a homemade device for fusing lights), and the infamous mask with "RAPIST" written large on its top section.

The next day, Mrs Hinton telephoned her daughter Flora, now back in London, and told her that on the news that morning the police had announced they had caught the rapist, and he was none other than their handyman Peter Cook. Flora thanked her lucky stars!

At the subsequent trial, it turned out Cook had, in the past, been convicted many times for burglary and had even served a five-year prison sentence on the last occasion.

Peter Cook received two life sentences for raping six women and wounding two others.

He died in HM Prison in Winchester in 2004 aged seventy-five.

The residents of Cambridge breathed a huge collective sigh of relief. There was now no possibility that Peter Cook could return and terrorise the female residents of Cambridge.

CHARIOTS OF FIRE AND TRINITY'S GREAT COURT RUN AND ANTI- SEMITISM CONTROVERSY (1981)

The classic David Puttnam film, *Chariots of Fire*, is an all-time classic, made in 1981, and ranked 19th in the list of top best 100 British films of all time.

Like many films of a historical nature, it changes the timing and emphasis for dramatic effect and the setting for some of the scenes.

The purpose of the film is to show the struggle two of Britain's athletes had in winning gold in the 1924 Olympics. Harold Abrahams was a Cambridge undergraduate, an English Jew, and Eric Liddell was a Scottish Christian missionary. The latter's struggle was the fact that his religious beliefs would not allow him to run on a Sunday, so he had to change his event from 100 metres to 400 metres.

Harold Abrahams, a law student at Gonville and Caius College Cambridge, was depicted as being obsessed with antiSemitism, forcing him to prove himself the best.

There was no question that the film greatly exaggerated the anti-Semitic feeling towards Abrahams.

Also, the film-makers found it irresistible not to use Trinity's Great Court Annual Run by freshers. The aim was to complete the run round the 300 metres or so of the Great Court before the clock on the King Edward III Tower had finished its 12 o'clock chime; about forty-three seconds. They had Harold Abrahams winning the race before the twelfth chime. In actual fact, Harold Abrahams never took part in the race. It was for this reason and not anti-Semitism that the Trinity authorities would not allow the film-makers to use the Great Court; it was filmed at Eton College instead.

Gonville and Caius College, Abrahams' alma mater, would not allow the film-makers in because of the anti-Semitic remarks made in the film by two of its senior dons; some of Gonville and Caius' greatest donors were Jewish.

Abrahams did win blues for representing Cambridge and winning in the long jump and sprint events.

He won a place in Great Britain's 1924 Olympic Squad and won a gold medal in the 100 metres.

Eric Liddell won gold in the 400 metres and immediately returned to China as a missionary; he died in 1945 in a Japanese concentration camp at the age of forty-three, towards the end of World War II.

Harold Abrahams spent a lifetime in the media as a journalist and a premier BBC Sports' commentator. He was a great Gilbert and Sullivan fan, marrying one of the D'Oyly Carte's principal singers Sybil Evers.

In 1934, he converted to Roman Catholicism.

One other detail the film-makers changed was the location of the British Olympic Training Camp. Instead of Broadstairs in Kent, they used St Andrews in Scotland, where the full squad was shown running across the full expanse of the beach, accompanied by Vangelis' wonderful "Chariots of Fire" theme.

CAMBRIDGE UNIVERSITY LIBRARY – GUARDIAN OF BRITAIN'S IMPERIAL PAST (1993)

In 1993, Cambridge University Library acquired the Royal Commonwealth Library, which had been held in London since 1848 when it was founded as the Colonial Institute Library and later the Royal Empire Society Library.

It is the largest collection of books, manuscripts, maps, photographs, pamphlets and periodicals relating to the British Empire anywhere in the world. It contains no less than 300,000 items, including 120,000 photographs, 8,500 titles on Australia, 2,500 on New Zealand and 6,000 on Canada. There are extensive records of the British Raj — successor to the British East India Company in India and Ceylon (modern day Sri Lanka) — including items appertaining to the history of tea and coffee plantations.

The collection is important because it is a record of the creation and growth of the largest empire the world has ever known. In its heyday in the early 1900s, the British Empire controlled over a quarter of the world and its population of 458 million. It shaped America and Australasia, ensuring that English became the most dominant language in the world.

Before the First World War, nobody questioned its legitimacy. It was a great civilising influence and example of Christian values. After all, it had always been there. Well, at least since the early days of the 17th century, through such trading conglomerates as the Virginia Company in America and the mighty British East India Company in the Near and Far East, with its own army, greater than the British Army. The latter drove out the French, Dutch and Portuguese, replacing their influence with the British ethos of fair play and good government.

And didn't we teach them all to play cricket, the epitome of civilised culture and fair play?

Writers like Rudyard Kipling and Rider Haggard extolled its virtues.

It was after the First World War that writers such as George Orwell (*Burmese Days*), Lytton Strachey (*Eminent Victorians*) and E. M. Forster (*Passage to India*) began shedding light on the true nature of the British Empire. Naked commercial exploitation through drug trafficking and the vast slave trade (until its abolition in the 19th century) leading the way. The native populations of these countries were exploited and subject to racial discrimination in its most extreme form.

Today, the concept of the British Empire evokes feelings of nostalgia and revulsion in equal measure. But it is, for good or bad, part of Britain's heritage and a vital part of the creation of the world we live in today.

The Royal Commonwealth Library is an important element in understanding the background to imperial Britain and one of the jewels of the Cambridge University Library.

MR BEAN VISITS THE FITZWILLIAM (2006)

If Rowan Atkinson's much-loved character Mr Bean was ever to visit a museum, the film script surely would follow much the same lines as the real-life scenario played out by the forty-two-year-old Cambridge resident Nick Flynn, when he visited the Fitzwilliam Museum in January 2006.

The unfortunate Mr Flynn was descending a staircase in the museum which was lined with window sills displaying valuable 17th century Chinese vases from the Qing dynasty, when he tripped on a loose shoelace. His six-foot, thirteen-stone frame was sent tumbling down the staircase and, with no handrail to grasp, he clutched at a window sill. Unfortunately, the window sill in question contained three 17th century Qing dynasty vases, which he managed to dislodge from their perch and they, in turn, joined Mr Flynn on his uncontrolled downwards journey. But, unlike their human travelling companion who escaped unharmed, they were shattered into smithereens.

This is a scenario of which one's wildest dreams are made, destroying valuable artefacts worth £500,000. Fortunately, the museum's insurance covered such an eventuality, so Nick Flynn escaped unscathed, both physically and financially.

However, four months later and after due consideration by the "powers that be", in true cops-and-robbers style, twenty-five policemen descended on Mr Flynn's home in a dawn raid. He was handcuffed and taken away to Cambridge Police Station, where he spent a day and night being interrogated on suspicion of mounting an elaborate publicity stunt which resulted in criminal damage. However, it soon became apparent that the church-going, law-abiding citizen was a frequent visitor to the Fitzwilliam and had never so much as knocked over a tea cup in the museum's restaurant. In short, he was a fine, upright (except for the downward fall in the museum) citizen and he was duly released.

However, the museum authorities wrote to him, advising that they would prefer if he did not visit the museum in future. Mr Flynn, with typical insouciance, felt this was a most ungrateful missive, as his escapade had attracted much media attention, and he felt that visitor numbers had, as a result, greatly increased. People, it would seem, were keen to see the three vases which had been painstakingly restored and were now on display again to the public. He felt that the least the museum authorities should do was to make him a trustee.

CORPUS CHRISTI'S TIME-EATER CLOCK (2008)

Whilst sundials have been a feature of Cambridge colleges since the 16th century, there are five still extant; horology has never seen anything quite like the Corpus grasshopper clock with its eponymous chronophage (time-eater) grasshopper.

Located on the corner of Benet Street and Trumpington Street, occupying what was once the entrance to a branch of NatWest bank which is now the Taylor Library, the golden splendour of the clock's dial face is an architectural masterpiece. It is one of Cambridge's most viewed tourist attractions since its installation in 2008.

At first sight, it is not obvious that it is a timepiece, neither resembling a conventional clock nor a sundial. On close inspection, it is the grim-looking metal sculpture of an insectoid creature similar to a grasshopper sitting on top of the five-foot diameter clock face that catches the eye. It moves its mouth, appearing to eat up the seconds as they pass, and occasionally it blinks in seeming satisfaction; but how does one discern the time?

The answer to that lies in the three rings on the clock face which each contain blue LEDs that shine behind. The outer ring denotes the seconds, the middle the minutes and the inner ring the hours.

THE CORPUS TIME EATER CLOCK

The Corpus clock was the brainchild of an old member of the college, John C. Taylor, who as well as funding the new Taylor Library invested one million pounds in his innovative clock. He wanted a clock that was like no other, which would be terrifying in appearance to demonstrate that time is not on our side, eating up every minute of our lives. It has been described as hypnotically beautiful and deeply disturbing.

John Taylor made his fortune designing and producing thermostats for kettles, but after retiring, he devoted five years to the Corpus Christi clock project, utilising 200 people including engineers, sculptors, scientists, jewellers and calligraphers, and employing the local engineering firm of Huxley Bertram.

Appropriately, the clock was unveiled on 19th September 2008 by Cambridge physicist Stephen Hawking, author of *A Brief History of Time*.

TRINITY COLLEGE'S VAST WINE COLLECTION (2010)

It is a well-known fact that Trinity College Cambridge is the wealthiest of all the Oxford and Cambridge colleges; its net worth exceeding £1.4 billion.

That is exactly what its founder, the hubristic Henry VIII, intended when he founded Trinity in 1546. He even closed down two existing colleges and transferred their buildings and other assets to his new college.

What is less well-known is the fact that Trinity possesses by far the most valuable wine collection of any Oxbridge college. In 2010, it was valued at over £1.7 million, comprising over 25,000 bottles including some bottles of 1978 Hermitage La Chapelle worth £650 a bottle. The second most valuable collection is held by Wadham College Oxford, worth £425,000.

To put this in perspective, the government's far-ranging holdings are valued at just over £2 million and the royal household's stock is also worth around £2 million.

Trinity's wines are usually reserved for the college fellows and honoured guests. However, the students get to partake on two occasions during their time at Trinity, at the Matriculation and Graduation Dinners, where they drink copiously of the finest wines. An experience which probably sets the benchmark for their future tastes as enlightened imbibers. So, don't ask a Trinity alumnus to dinner! For Trinity's wines are also of the finest quality.

OTHER PLACES NAMED CAMBRIDGE (2021)

There are no less than thirty-eight places in the world named Cambridge, in six different countries, twenty-five in America alone. There are also four in Jamaica, two in Canada, one in South Africa, one in Australia, one in New Zealand and four in the United Kingdom. The most prestigious outside the UK is undoubtedly Cambridge, Massachusetts, home to Harvard University.

Collectively, Cambridge and Oxford, home to the United Kingdom's two oldest and most prestigious universities, are known as "Oxbridge", but this is a comparatively recent term, first appearing in Thackeray's novel *Pendennis* in 1849. Oxbridge was a fictional university in one place whilst the other was Camford. Quite why Oxbridge has caught on and is part of everyday jargon and Camford has not, has something to do with phonetics, and it is now known as a portmanteau word ("smog" and "brunch" are other examples) which is a morphological blend. Interestingly, the real Oxbridge is a hamlet in Dorset. There does not appear to be a place called Camford.

Cambridge in England was not granted the title and dignity of a city until the 24th March 1951, some 800 years after its great rival, Oxford. Even its American eponym, the cradle of Harvard University, was granted city status over 100 years before its English namesake. Part of the reason is its essential provincial nature away from the pathway of kings and armies on their way to London, and the fact that it does not possess a cathedral, being part of the Diocese of Ely whose bishops had a huge influence on the development of Cambridge University in its early days.

Today, there is no doubting Cambridge's pre-eminence, as it is now the administrative centre of a much enlarged Cambridgeshire, which since 1974 has included Huntingdonshire and Peterborough.

Also, Cambridge University, until 2011, had as its chancellor the Duke of Edinburgh, who was in office for thirty-five years, the third longest of any chancellor of either of our great universities and certainly the most prestigious.

CAMBRIDGE'S UNMATCHED SCULPTURE COLLECTION (2022)

Cambridge's collection of over 2,000 items of sculpture is unmatched in Britain, with the exception of London.

Every aspect of human endeavour is commemorated, from Greek scholars, Socrates and Homer; scientists, Isaac Newton and William Cavendish; politicians, including William Pitt the Younger; and a multitude of kings and queens, including Edward III, Henry VIII and Queen Elizabeth I. The list is endless.

There is a treasure trove of art here, all accessible to the public; noted sculptors such as Hepworth, Thorvaldsen, Roubiliac, Westmacott, the controversial Eric Gill and many more.

The Fitzwilliam Museum is an obvious starting point, as it contains works by Degas, Rodin, Epstein and Moore. Statues from the ancient Egyptian period and from a little later, including a wonderful statue of Alexander the Great carved in about 100 BC. It is estimated that there are over 700 items of statuary in the Fitzwilliam alone.

Trinity College has the best collection of statues of any college. Its many gateways contain statues of its founder, Henry VIII, and four other monarchs. Its chapel and Wren Library contain over fifty busts of statues, including Plato, Virgil, Ben Johnson, Inigo Jones and, of course, Trinity's most famous alumnus, Isaac Newton (1642–1726), who has a bust in the Wren Library and a statue by Roubiliac in the antechapel.

Cambridge graduate and arguably Britain's greatest statesman, William Pitt the Younger (1759–1806) has two statues as well: one in the university Senate House by Joseph Nollekens, and the other outside the library of his alma mater, Pembroke College, seated in a toga and sandals. He became prime minister at the age of twenty-four, which office he occupied for twenty years; unmatched before or since.

Probably the most recognisable statue in Cambridge is the jaunty soldier portrayed on the War Memorial initially installed at the end of Station Road. Unveiled in 1922, it shows a bare-headed soldier with a laurel wreath and German helmet slung over his rifle. Not at all like the sombre note struck by most war memorials. It is probably Tait McKenzie's most famous sculpture. It was moved to a location close to the Botanic Gardens in 1996.

Statues are no longer in vogue so Cambridge must treasure its priceless collection and make the public aware of their accessibility.

CAMBRIDGES UNUSUAL WAR MEMORIAL

UNKNOWN
CAMBRIDGE

Printed in Great Britain
by Amazon

36379405R00154